HAUNTED
BLACK COUNTRY

HAUNTED

BLACK COUNTRY

PHILIP SOLOMON

This book is dedicated to my mother, Elsie, who taught me well that there is more to life than just this one, and that, 'Death may hide but not divide, they are but on God's other side'.

Frontispiece: This photograph was donated to the author and is a good example of what was presented to be spirit photography in the past.

First published 2009

The History Press
The Mill, Brimscombe Port
Stroud, Gloucestershire, GL5 2QG
www.thehistorypress.co.uk

Reprinted 2010

ISBN 978 0 7524 4882 4

Typesetting and origination by The History Press
Printed in Great Britain

CONTENTS

INTRODUCTION

I decided to write this book after many people contacted me to tell me of their own experiences with ghosts and haunted buildings throughout the Black Country area of the West Midlands. It is not surprising, as for many years I have not only been a feature writer for *Psychic News*, but I am also the Psychic Agony Uncle for the UK's biggest circulated evening newspaper, the *Wolverhampton Express & Star*. Almost everyone in the Black Country has the *Star* (as the paper is affectionately known) delivered to their home.

Hopefully, as one of Britain's most respected Spiritualist mediums and the author of several books on the subject, I have learned to sort the chaff from the wheat or, as you might prefer to call it, the tall stories from the genuine reports of paranormal occurrences. Almost all of the stories you will read in this book have been personally investigated by

The author demonstrating clairvoyance at one of his many events up and down the UK.

me or my team of professional researchers, and one or two of them have been told on Wolverhampton City Radio (WCR), where I present The Philip Solomon Fifties and Sixties Show every Monday evening between 7 p.m. and 9 p.m. However, many of these stories have remained untold until this book was written and will reveal where they are to be seen, heard and witnessed in the area known as the Black Country, a place claimed by many to be the most haunted region in the world.

In my opinion, ghosts are generally just the remains of memories – usually of people – who died rather tragically and are unaware of their own death, or passing over as I really prefer to call it. A ghost is part of a person's personality left earthbound in the atmosphere of their former existence, and usually appears in the same place over and over again. Ghosts rarely travel any distance at all and never, at least in my experience, leave the immediate area of their passing over. However, spirits can, and indeed do, move around and travel.

Ghosts and spirits are not the same thing. Spirits are the surviving personalities of all of us when we progress past death to a higher sphere where we continue to progress in an existence where we act out our lives, receive care, and give and take love, much as we do in this life, except that it is in another higher dimension. A ghost, however, can only relive and repeat, over and over again, the final moments of his or her life in a tormented and repetitive obsession, locked to the earth plane in a totally benighted state. They are quite incapable of progressing to the higher life and are also, may I say here and now, nearly always completely harmless.

Although there is usually nothing to fear from a ghost, it is possible that a strange or rather unpleasant entity could be drawn to your vibration and you could encounter something the experts call 'not quite nice'. Any time you consider yourself not to be completely and totally in control, immediately stop what you are doing and pass the investigation on to a professional medium. If you don't know a medium I would suggest that you get in touch with your local Spiritualist church. There will certainly be people there who will be able to help.

Ghosts in the majority of cases, when they are able to draw energy from the living, are especially likely to make themselves known where one or more persons with psychic ability are present and capable of hearing or seeing an apparition. It may also cause certain phenomena or movement of objects, such as a glass or the opening or closing of a door. When the manifestation becomes purely physical in its nature and can be observed by most people, it could possibly be that a poltergeist haunting is underway. However, if you look closely, it is well known that adolescents approaching or passing through puberty have untapped energies, right and ripe to cause poltergeist-type activity. It has been strongly hypothesised that the sexual fluids are similar, if not identical, to the so-called ectoplasm produced by the physical medium in controlled séances, and is supposed to attract ghosts like bees to a honey pot. Remember I have told you that they are quite unable to accept their transition to the higher life generally and remain here. Some of them can be a little naughty, just as they were naughty in their earthly life, and they are the type of people, if they are proper poltergeists, who may cause a few problems.

One false tale concerning ghosts is that they only come out at night. I can assure you that you are just as likely to see one in broad daylight as in the dark hours of night. However, atmosphere is important and the less noise and disturbance there is, the more likely they are to communicate or appear. I also suggest that you have a look at dates, anniversaries of deaths and similar instances, since they may have made an indelible imprint in time and atmosphere alike, and ghosts do not go away with passing time. They are locked in limbo for eternity; that is unless someone such as a trance medium contacts them and can convince them of their passing. However, this is usually done over a period of time and in a controlled rescue circle and should not be attempted by amateurs and never, ever on your own!

An interesting point to note; where you see 'Normal or Paranormal?' at the end of some of the stories in this book you will find a short explanation for possible normal and paranormal reasons for an occurrence, which may be of help to the reader when considering possible 'supernatural' causes.

'Hmm, now this could be interesting', says the author, taking a closer look.

A BRIEF HISTORY OF THE BLACK COUNTRY

The Black Country is an area of the West Midlands, to the north and west of Birmingham, and to the south and east of Wolverhampton, around the South Staffordshire coalfield. By the late nineteenth century, this area had become one of the most industrialised in the whole of the UK. The Staffordshire coal mines, iron foundries and steel mills that used the local coal to fire their furnaces produced very bad pollution.

It is popularly believed the Black Country got its name because of the black soot that covered the area as a result of the heavy industry that took place there and legend has it that Queen Victoria ordered the blinds on the windows in her carriage to be closed as the royal train steamed through the area. But it is likely that the name existed even before the Industrial Revolution came to the Black Country and was relevant to the presence of coal being mined near the surface, causing the soil to be very black.

The Black Country is also famous for its unusual and distinctive dialect, which is spoken slightly differently in various parts of the region. Despite being close to Birmingham, Black Country people do not have a close affiliation or see themselves as part of Birmingham, and are very proud of their own Black Country identity as a totally separate area. The boundaries of the Black Country are, however, a matter for conjecture among local historians, some believing all of Wolverhampton is included, but not others. A twenty-first-century definition of the Black Country links the four Metropolitan Boroughs of Dudley, Sandwell, Walsall and Wolverhampton. The ancient town of Dudley, again controversially, is sometimes referred to by some historians as the capital of the Black Country.

The Black Country is within the West Midlands county, but at one time was divided between the counties of Staffordshire and Worcestershire. At one time, Dudley was a detached part of Worcestershire within Staffordshire, and some still speak of Dudley being within Worcestershire, whereas the ancient parish of Halesowen, which included Warley and Oldbury, but not Cradley, was actually part of the old Salop and Shropshire counties. It includes parts of the city of Wolverhampton, and the towns of Bilston, Blackheath, Brierley Hill, Coseley, Cradley, Darlaston, Dudley, Gornal, Great Bridge, Halesowen, Lye, Netherton, Oldbury, Quarry Bank, Rowley Regis, Sedgley, Stourbridge, Tipton, Walsall, Warley, Wednesbury, Wednesfield, West Bromwich, Willenhall, and Wordsley.

Industrialisation in the Black Country goes way back in history, for it was already an area where metal working was important as far back as the sixteenth century, due to the presence of iron ore and coal, and many people supplemented their living with agricultural smallholdings by working as nailers or smiths, an example of a phenomenon known to economic historians as proto-industrialisation.

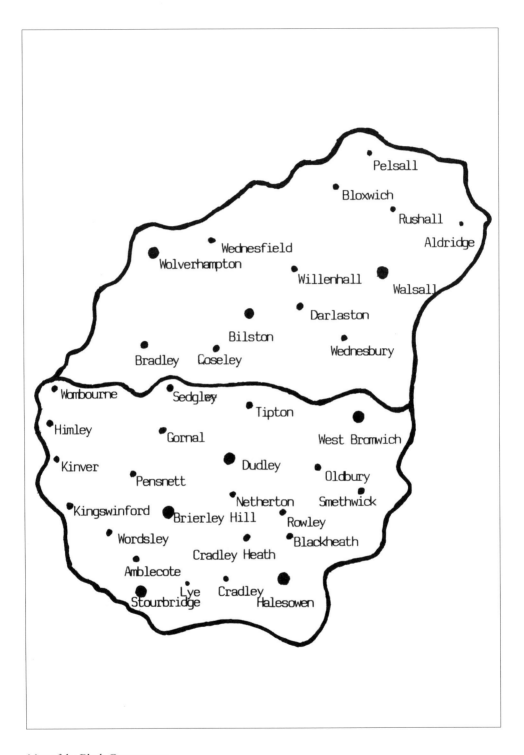

Map of the Black Country area.

Before the Industrial Revolution came about, coal and limestone were mined and used locally and in fairly small quantities, but with the opening of canals and advances in the use of coke in the production of iron, this saw the area expand very quickly. By Victorian times, the Black Country was one of the most heavily industrialised areas in Britain, and it became known for its pollution, particularly from iron and coal industries and their many associated smaller businesses. This led to the expansion of local railways and coal mine lines.

The area became notorious following the publication by Charles Dickens' *The Old Curiosity Shop*, written in 1841, which described how the area's local factory chimneys, 'Poured out their plague of smoke, obscured the light, and made foul the melancholy air'. Some even claim that J.R.R. Tolkien based Mordor in his novel, *The Lord of the Rings*, on the heavily industrialised Black Country area. Indeed, in the Elvish Sindarin language, Mor-Dor means Black Land and is sometimes even referred to within the novel as 'the Black Country' itself.

The heavy industry which once dominated the Black Country has now largely gone. Mining completely ceased in the area in the late 1960s and pollution guidelines to industry means that the Black Country is no longer black. The area still has some manufacturing, but on a much smaller scale than in the past. Luckily, the Black Country Living Museum in Dudley preserves and presents life in the Black Country in the early twentieth century and is a popular tourist attraction.

The strong Black Country dialect is less frequently heard today than in the past. However, a stronger variation of the dialect can still be heard amongst some older Black Country people, and many do take a great pride in preserving the history in the way they speak (or spake). The author writes a weekly column in the *Express & Star* in traditional Black Country dialect, which is popular among the local population and is even used by many of the local schools, colleges and universities to present examples to their students and those from outside the area.

Word endings with 'in' are still noticeable in conversation, such as gooin' for going, callin' for calling, etc. Other pronunciations are 'fer' for far or for, and 'loff' for laugh, which is extremely similar to Chaucer's use of English. A good example of the use of the dialect can be seen in the story about the Tipton Slasher and the prediction of his downfall by the so-called Dudley Devil, Theophillus Dunn.

The Black Country has four radio stations. The author is a presenter at Wolverhampton City Radio (WCR) and often invites people from the paranormal or psychic world as guests on the show. Beacon Radio and Wolverhampton has its own local station called The Wolf.

The *Wolverhampton Express & Star* is the region's top newspaper and the author is a feature writer for them. They publish eleven local editions from their Wolverhampton headquarters (for example the Dudley edition will have a different front page to the Wolverhampton or Stafford editions). Incidentally, the *Express & Star*, traditionally a Black Country newspaper, has expanded to the point where they sell copies right across the West Midlands.

THE GHOST HUNTER'S TOOLKIT

Any parapsychologist or those interested in looking for ghosts will tell you the one thing you must have if you are to successfully investigate this area of the paranormal is a completely open mind. This is of great importance, for whenever I have been involved in this kind of research and accompanied by the type of individual or group who clearly believe before they start that they are not going to see, sense, or find anything at all that could be considered paranormal, they generally don't. By the same principle, don't undertake such investigations whilst convinced that you are definitely going to see something; that is an open invitation to your mind and its unconscious levels to start playing tricks on you, and you will see and hear things that are not there. Also, be very careful not to insist that something is paranormal before all investigations have taken place to see if it is actually only normal in context.

What I would suggest to the reader is this: if you are actually interested in finding out about ghosts in the Black Country, why not consider getting together a little ghost hunter's kit that would help you greatly in finding out whether or not somewhere really is haunted. People may suggest you need such things as meters to measure electro-magnetic field changes, heat-sensing cameras, special thermometers, and a whole plethora of fancy equipment that in my experience as a ghost hunter is really of very little use. All you really need are simple items which you can gather generally from around your home or local hardware store.

What you will need is a good camera, and this really should be a 35mm film camera which, if at all possible, has an infra-red lock on it. Photographs produced with digital cameras today can so easily be manipulated that almost no self-respecting investigator of the paranormal has any interest in them. Also, just use a very simple camcorder, but preferably one that can film in quite low light. You don't need an expensive camcorder and again I must inform you that most of the so-called orbs that are produced and presented as ghosts or other unusual phenomena are actually no more than the usual dust particles in the air that are picked up by most camcorders when recording in the dark.

Below is a very simple kit for you to get together which I suggest would be more than acceptable to any ghost hunter in the Black Country, or anywhere else for that matter, together with a simple explanation of the uses for each object.

A Ghost Hunter's Toolkit

1. Notepad
2. Pen and pencil
3. Retractable ruler
4. 12in ruler
5. Watch – digital, nightlight
6. Magnifying glass
7. Spool of black cotton
8. String
9. Tape recorder
10. Contact adhesive – 1in tape
11. Powerful torch
12. Thermometer
13. Packet of chalks
14. Talcum powder and 1in paintbrush
15. Pencil sharpener
16. Camera – with a built-in flash
17. Video camera
18. Spare batteries

A notepad, pens and pencils are vital for making notes of anything that happens. Note exactly and absolutely factually any occurrences or sounds that are heard. Also note whether they were witnessed by someone else apart from you. Time and date should also be recorded precisely. You will find the magnifying glass of immeasurable use when looking at footprints and handprints; they may be invisible to the human eye but you will see them through your glass. It can also be used for examining traces of post-ghostly substances left behind.

The talcum powder and the paintbrush can also be useful in conjunction with the magnifying glass. For example, if you shake the talc onto a cupboard, a chair, a table or anything with a polished surface, then gently blow it away, it will leave the impression of any prints, natural or supernatural, that are there. Now should that print not match any of those of the residents or visitors, you've got your first winner and are learning the tricks of the trade of ghost hunting!

Now let's move to your chalks – you can use them to mark around movable objects such as chairs or table legs which have perhaps been reported to move around on their own. It may involve a long sitting on your part but if you have chalked it and it moves, you've got another winner, haven't you? The string, self-adhesive tape and cotton are for securing and sealing doors and windows. Far and away the best of the three, in my opinion, is the self-adhesive tape. For example, use about four or five pieces cut at about 3in and place them on the doors and frames which are reported as self-opening; set up your watch; the evidence of any breakage of the tape will be obvious.

A tape recorder is also a most useful tool for anyone researching the existence of ghosts and should accompany you on every investigation if at all possible. I would also suggest that you buy some extra batteries for it – the type that can be recharged time and time again. (Actually you should always carry a spare set of batteries for everything.) They are an excellent investment and I do suggest that your tape recorder should always be on record at all times. However, be on your guard, for there is usually a natural explanation for most sounds.

Investing in a good camera is absolutely vital. I stress good rather than expensive and the fewer requirements for adjustment of controls the better. It should incorporate an infra-red focus lock if at all possible and, at the time of writing this book, the type of camera I have described can be purchased for less than a hundred pounds. This is indeed the simple type of camera I use, and I find the infra-red lock and built-in flash invaluable at night. A video camera is also an excellent piece of equipment to take on any investigation with you, but I do suggest that you explain to the supplier exactly what you want to use it for; some video cameras in my experience are much better than others for filming in the dark. If you want more technical equipment the following is a list of items that might prove useful to you above and beyond the simple kit I have suggested.

An electro-magnetic field detector (often referred to as an EMF meter) is a piece of equipment that can detect the presence of electro-magnetic fields. There are many today who believe these fields can be caused by ghosts and picked up around haunted buildings, but do remember they also pick up measurements from televisions, electrical wiring, and other equipment, so keep this in mind if you use them. Also get one where the measurement is displayed for you, i.e. 2.5 to 2.10 milli-gauss, or one that has a needle that gives a reading. You really want one that displays in the dark too. The very cheap ones that just beep or flash red or green when a ghost is allegedly present will not be much use to you.

A 35mm film camera would really be the advised piece of equipment even over digital cameras. Anyone who examines your photographic evidence of ghosts will tend to be less prepared to accept it in digital format. Use the very best film you can afford: my personal recommendation would be Kodak Gold 400-speed film, which gets the best all-round results in my view, although some favour 800 or 200-speed film. One problem you should be aware of: pictures taken at night or in the dark with very fast shutter speed can be quite grainy and unclear. You may wish to take advantage of using infra-red film but note that, although it can be an excellent way to work at haunted sites, it can be quite expensive to purchase and these days very expensive to develop too.

You might like to purchase a digital thermometer which will give you the capability to measure such areas as cold spots. If you do get one, one that has a highest and lowest temperature memory and an alarm too would be the best to purchase. A better, but more expensive option would be a thermal scanner which uses infra-red technology to immediately register temperature changes at a distance – not a cheap item, but a piece of equipment that can be extremely useful.

If you can afford a night-vision camera, this works in much the same way as equipping your ordinary video camera with a night-vision scope which will record light and the way it changes much more accurately and even pick up light that you cannot see with your own eyes. Many parapsychologists today use night-vision scopes. They probably have their uses in a dark churchyard or unlit lane perhaps, but they are pricey items that some people consider to be not really worth purchasing unless you can afford the very best.

Thermal imaging scopes can be used to measure temperature changes that happen in front of you and they will also give you the ability to actually see what your thermal scanner 'sees', making use of infra-red technology so that not only can you look on a cold spot you can actually see the form and shape it takes. Again, an expensive piece of equipment but if you are serious about ghost hunting, one that could be very valuable.

Digital tape recorders have now become the must-have item for recording electronic voice phenomena and no one could really discount their value. Massive amounts of audio can be stored on these little machines and the quality is brilliant, though personally I always liked the old standard audio tape recorder and separate microphone to be used as well but then that is probably me being a traditionalist.

Good-quality motion detectors can be useful equipment if used in the right hands. They will certainly tell you if there has been movement somewhere where it should not have taken place. These sorts of equipment can be useful when set up across a room, corridor, or even stairs, and allow you to check out and monitor quite large spaces with just one simple-to-set-up device. They have certainly become a lot cheaper to buy now and can be a very useful ghost hunter's tool, especially for indoor work.

I advised you right at the start of this chapter to get together a simple toolkit which I have outlined for you. I still stand by this as the basic equipment that you will require in the early days of your interest in investigating the paranormal. As you get more serious about your work, perhaps you would like to add the other equipment and never-ending supply of devices on offer to detect ghosts to your personal toolkit. Good luck to you and I wish you only happy ghost hunting!

DO YOUR EYES LIE TO YOU ON OCCASION?

The answer is most definitely yes, and you should be aware of this fact when checking out ghosts and the paranormal generally. For the most part, our eyes serve us extremely well and send true visions back to the brain. However, there are times when one's visual perception of things are not always as they seem. Many psychologists have turned to illusions in which perceptions of things are confusing and misleading, to get a better knowledge and understanding of the process. For years many scientists have studied geometrical illusions and, despite various individuals hypothesising explanations, to be quite honest, no one can fully explain how they work. It is important that you are aware of these facts (or tricks of the eyes, if you like). You should also know that some illusions are based on relative size in contrast to surroundings.

I do not wish to over-elaborate or go into the technical details of what I have just stated, but it should be remembered that we live in a world of people and objects that bombard our senses with constant stimulation and on a conscious level we are not always completely aware of it unless, to give an example, we are sitting in the dark when suddenly a flash of light appears and immediately gains our individual attention. That would be a single stimulus and when we concentrate on a single stimulus, all sorts of things can happen.

You should take into consideration other factors, such as was what I saw a true revelation, a trick of the light, or even what it seemed to be? A rumpled curtain, for example, can become a face; a fox's eyes on a country road can be interpreted in all sorts of ways if we let our imagination run riot. Things are not always as we see them and you must always be aware of this fact and not turn something into what you think it is rather than what it actually is. Remember – sometimes our eyes do indeed deceive us.

Here is an interesting little experiment for you to try. Below is a reproduction of a negative. Look very hard at the nose without blinking and count to 100 then immediately look at the ceiling or wall – white if possible. I promise you, you will see something very positive if you keep looking, but don't forget; it could be your eyes telling you lies again, couldn't it?

Do your eyes lie? Take the test.

PART ONE

HAUNTED BLACK COUNTRY

Was Jack the Ripper a Black Country villain?

Over many years as an investigator of the paranormal and a professional medium, I have come across cases where people describe a particular ghost as being like, or whom they perceive to be, Jack the Ripper. Until a séance in 2007, which I was involved in, I always considered this most unlikely because, of course, all of the murders took place in the Whitechapel area of London. However, I have been forced to reassess this conclusion.

David Jones of Dudley told me he saw a ghost he emphatically believed to be the Ripper in Hill Street, Stourbridge, whereas Mary Robinson told me she had seen such a character she also believed to be a ghost in the area of Bilston Market. Another correspondent who wishes to remain anonymous said they had seen the spectre of Jack the Ripper, or possibly Palmer the Poisoner, in Wolverhampton.

So how does my séance in 2007 and these visions fit in? Well, during that séance, a certain William Bury came through and insisted he was indeed the Ripper and that he was sorry for what he had done. However, he also claimed that people of an extremely high aristocratic background with connections to Dudley were also involved and had made him take part in the killings, thus intimating that he had been instructed or blackmailed into killing certain girls in London.

A little bit of research into Bury's background is fascinating. He was actually born in Stourbridge on 25 May 1859, in, of all places, Hill Street, according to some records. Not too much can be found about his early life but records do suggest his mother, Mary, had been confined to a lunatic asylum, where she ultimately died. Bury's father was an honest, hard-working man, claimed to be a fishmonger by some and a butcher by others. The youngest of several children, it is said his father taught him to cut and butcher meat and fish to a professional standard. It is also said Bury did not like the trade and this led him to move to London, but not before returning back to the Black Country to live in Wolverhampton with an uncle for a while, where he made a living selling items obtained by dubious means, although others suggest he sold items such as pencils, pens and small items of jewellery. Bilston Market would have been a favourite haunt for hawking such products in those days.

Bored with his life, at twenty-eight he returned to London and got a job driving a sawdust cart and met and married Ellen Elliot, a barmaid and prostitute. Ellen was described by all and sundry as a pleasant, if misguided soul and, although she operated within the oldest profession of them all, had actually been left a legacy of £300, a small fortune in those days.

Was Jack the Ripper a Black Country
Villain? (Courtesy of Graham Walsh)

The newly-weds settled down in Bow in the East End of London in comfortable lodgings. Within five days of their marriage some records suggest William Bury had to be restrained from cutting his wife's throat with a table knife after some minor dispute. Research suggests Ellen had an unhappy life and Bury would hurt her and anyone else if crossed.

After being sacked by his employer, James Martin, the couple brought their own sawdust company into being, but most of the money was spent on bad women and drink by William. But was he Jack the Ripper? In a final effort to make their relationship work, despite advice from family and friends, the couple moved to Dundee in Scotland to start a new life. He did not change his ways and police reports suggest that on 10 February 1889 William Henry Bury went into Bell Street police station and claimed: 'I am Jack the Ripper and I want to give myself up'. He told the police that if they went to his house in Princes Street they would find the body of a woman cut up in a box. Despite believing him to be intoxicated or a madman, the police duly visited the address and indeed found Ellen's body twisted and contorted inside a box. A long-bladed knife lay nearby with strands of Ellen's hair still attached to it. Investigation of the corpse suggest she had been strangled, and her body mutilated by a knife wound from the pubic bone up towards the stomach, from which 12in of intestine were hanging. There were a total of nine incisions made by the knife to other parts of her body. Strangely enough, despite all the evidence, during his trial Bury pleaded not guilty to the murder and genuinely believed he had a chance of reprieve. Many believed this would involve him naming other people to the police associated with horrible murders, although this claim has never been proven. Bury was also refused permission to speak in his own defence at the trial.

The jury quickly returned a verdict of guilty and on the morning of his execution he enjoyed a breakfast of bread and butter, poached eggs and other favourite things, thanked all present for their kindness and said to the warder who was to lead him to the scaffold, 'I forgive all who have given false evidence against me and hope God will forgive me'. He was hanged on 24 April 1889, at 8 o'clock in the morning. Just before his execution, when hangman Berry tried to obtain a confession from Bury for the Whitechapel slayings, Bury is claimed to have said, 'I suppose you think you are clever to hang me but you are not going to get anything out of me.' Although he didn't confess, the hangman was convinced that he had hung Jack the Ripper. Bury certainly fitted descriptions of the murderer: he was 5ft 3in tall, weighed just under 10st, was good looking with dark features and often wore a moustache.

We know Bury certainly came to Wolverhampton – possibly to holiday with family who lived there – and that one of the victims, Catherine 'Kate' Eddowes, a lady of the night, was also from Wolverhampton. But did Bury definitely tell us he was the Ripper at that séance? He actually gave us the same answer he gave James Berry, 'I'm not telling you'. There is still research to do, but it is fact that a case could be made for William Bury being Jack the Ripper and many of you have seen what you believe to be the ghost or shade of Jack the Ripper in several areas of the Black Country. Spookily fascinating, isn't it?

The Earl and the Gypsy Princess

This story is just as much a love story as a ghost story, and tells of a love-bond so strong it broke the chains of the strongest class structure of its day. On certain summer nights a handsome, proud Earl and his lovely Romany girl can be seen walking hand-in-hand on the summits of Kinver Edge, forever bound in a love that not even death could break. This was their story in life.

In 1850, George 'Harry' Grey was twenty-three years old, the 7th Earl of Stanford and Warrington. Acclaimed amongst his ancestral line were Lady Jane Grey and others of similar nobility. He also owned many estates – Enville being one of them – and on top of all this he was fabulously rich, inheriting two earldoms and £90,000 per annum. As if this were not enough for one man, he was also lucky enough to be tall, fair and very handsome. The villages of Enville and nearby Kinver are in fact just inside the Staffordshire border, but have always been popular places for Black Country folk to visit and in many ways are very much associated with the Black Country.

At this stage I would like to take you away from Enville and the Black Country, to a little village in Dorset called Sturminster Marshall and the birth of a baby girl christened Catherine Cox, the daughter of a farm labourer and a gypsy mother. The girl's childhood proved to be very tragic. Her father was killed in an accident and her mother left her and her brothers and sisters to return to a life on the road. Catherine and two of her sisters, Susan and Polly, made their way to London and settled within the company of one Jem Mason, a famous horse trainer and dealer – well known by gypsies and aristocracy alike.

The three sisters were beautiful and hard-working, and quickly learned all they could about horses and riding, in the hope to procure work in the many circuses of that time, perhaps as show riders by night and fortune tellers by day. Before long, however, Catherine's beautiful face and figure were to catch the roving eye of one Percy Fielding, son of the Earl of Denbeigh, and they fell hopelessly in love (at least Catherine did) and, in 1854, a baby girl was born to them, also to be called Catherine. Captain Fielding, as he was now called, was sent off to the war between Britain and Russia by his family, and Catherine waved goodbye to the little cottage she had occupied for a short while, returning to London and Jem Mason, with a baby in her arms and precious little else!

I now return to the life of Harry Grey of Enville, local hero and sportsman. He was known by the great-grandparents of many of today's readers, for he excelled at cricket, boxing and horsemanship and often arranged and took part in contests with the locals just as willingly as with the famous. (By now he was a widower, having lost his dear wife, Bessie.) One day he travelled to London to visit the stables of Jem Mason to take a look at a couple of young horses that had been recommended to him by friends in the racing world. It was not to be a horse that would catch the lord's eye that day, however, but the girl that put the animals through their paces and various exercises, Catherine Cox, the most beautiful girl he had ever seen. Harry Grey was utterly and totally smitten and after a whirlwind romance the pair were wed.

Catherine was immediately sent to her husband's less well-known relatives for instruction and polish as befitted a Countess. Twelve months later, Lord Stanford presented his wife to Enville. Unfortunately, it has to be said that she was never accepted as a Lady, let alone a Countess by many of the Earl's family, friends and acquaintances. She was, however, much-loved by the common people, tenant workers and servants, showing concern and sympathy to them when times were hard, and many told a story of a kindly gift of food or money. She was also sympathetic towards petty criminals. It was noted on one occasion that she pleaded for clemency from her husband for a young man who had stolen flowers from the garden of the Great Hall.

The marriage itself proved to be a very happy one and it was said that Lord Grey never regretted marrying Catherine, and she in turn grew to love deeply a man whose attitude at times could be brash and arrogant. The Earl was also very kind to Catherine's relatives, allowing many of them to live at his various homes and retreats, and, although it was said this was done to relieve his wife's loneliness, it was still an honourable gesture.

The Earl had one major fault however; he was not wise with money. This fault, aligned with a wish to be seen as the king of the racing fraternity, and perhaps his judgment of bloodstock not being on a par with his riding ability, led to him paying out huge sums of money and ultimately losing a fortune. This, along with other escapades, led him so much into debt that eventually he had to raise a mortgage on the property he owned to make ends meet. The Countess, despite her utter dismay at his foolhardy ways, stayed as loyal to him when almost everything had gone as when he had been fabulously rich.

The Earl died in 1883 without issue, and the earldom passed to a cousin in South Africa. However, the village of Enville was willed to Catherine for life. Bereft and almost bankrupt, Catherine did not complain. Instead, she rolled up her sleeves and vowed to pay off Enville's debts incurred by the spendthrift Earl, or die in the attempt. Unbelievably, with good management and by opening and making accessible the estate to the Black Country's weekend visitors, to some extent she did, but, as was usual in Catherine's life, one more tragedy struck and Enville Hall was decimated by fire in 1904. The Countess never really recovered from the shock and passed away two months later. She had, however, lit the spark of recovery, and ten years after her death the Enville Estate was once more solvent and profitable.

Catherine never told the Earl about the baby girl she had before she met him, knowing that a man of his station, honour and position, would never come to terms with the

The Earl and Gypsy Princess.
(Courtesy of Graham Walsh)

situation. It was well known to the locals though that she had secretly brought the little girl to Enville and had her nursed and looked after by a lady whom she trusted to hold her tongue.

While they lived, the Earl and the Countess never had any children of their own, but doted on Catherine's niece and nephew. The Countess also doted on a girl who lived not far from the rectory in a little cottage with a single lady. That little girl, being well-educated, later married the Revd Alfred Payne, rector of Enville. I do not intend to identify the girl further, for I believe that her ancestry is obvious. Upon the death of the Countess, the estate passed to another Catherine. She was the daughter of Sarah Leticia, who in turn was the daughter of Tamar, sister of the Countess. The young Catherine had much pleased her great-aunt and the Earl by marrying the nephew of the Duke of Montrose. The couple later changed their name to Grey and for historians of the Black Country that is the same man (Sir Henry Foley Grey) who was the first Mayor of Stourbridge in 1914.

Many years have passed by since those days and Enville, to some extent, has slipped into a semi-rural background, taking a back seat to Kinver as a Mecca to visitors from the more populated Black Country conurbations, but there are many descendants of the people who lived in those times who will know of this story. So the next time your children are praising some love story they have seen on the television or silver screen, remind them of one of the truly great love stories that happened just down the road on the edge of the Black Country and, as I told you in the very first paragraph, the story is a serial that still goes on even today – according to some folk at least!

Caldmore's Hand of Glory and the Vanishing Sword

Let me take you back to the dark, gloomy streets of Caldmore Green, or plain 'Carmer' as the locals call it. The year was 1870 and a grisly discovery had just been made at the White Hart public house; a find that was believed to show evidence of a history of evil deeds practised locally, namely, the use of a 'Hand of Glory', a horrifying charm used by sorcerers and thieves.

It consisted of the hand and lower arm of a hanged criminal, cut off while the body was still suspended from the gallows. It was then dried and preserved in a secret pickling solution believed to include vinegar and salts. The hand was then finally set in a format to hold a candle made from the fat of the dead man's body, virgin wax and Lapland sesame. The abominable object was then said to have many magical powers. Thieves, for example, believed that when the candle was lit, they could enter any building at night, rifle its contents and anyone in residence would remain quite asleep until they left.

There is also the legend of a sword, which, so I am told, belonged to a very old Staffordshire family and dated from the times of Charles I. Again, the sword is said to have had many magical properties – so mystical in fact, that it would seem to have vanished without trace! However, I was told in absolute confidence in 1979 by the descendants of a family who had connections to Bradley Hall in Kingswinford around 1800, that the sword was still in the possession of distant family members and, who knows, perhaps one day I'll tell that story in full. For those with a morbid sense of curiosity, however, the arm may be seen by appointment at Walsall library.

Caldmore's Hand of Glory
and the Vanishing Sword.

The White Hart public house.

But the story does not end there – far from it! According to many people, particularly locals, several ghosts haunt the White Hart. The *Walsall Observer* carried a report about the landlord finding the strange print of a small hand in the loft in 1955, which, according to him, could not have been made by anyone living, for no one to the best of his knowledge had been in the loft. Another landlord claimed that on one occasion he heard footsteps above him. As he approached the stairs that led to the loft he looked up and noticed the door was slightly ajar; at that moment his German Shepherd dog stood bolt-upright, his fur standing on end. He called the dog away and ran down the stairs. He is reported to have told witnesses that not even an offer of £1,000 would persuade him to venture into the loft again!

There is also a well-known local legend of the White Hart being haunted by the ghost of a young lassie who committed suicide well over a century ago, and whom has reputedly appeared on a regular basis ever since. Whether these hauntings are relevant to the magical properties of the sword or the so-called 'Hand of Glory' will perhaps forever remain a matter for conjecture and hypothesis, but one fact that cannot be denied is that the White Hart most definitely has a certain atmosphere.

At the time of writing (2008), it is unfortunate to report that the White Hart has been extensively damaged by fire. However, in my experience fire cannot hurt or remove ghosts, nor banish legends, and I am sure many more stories will unfold before all the questions that remain unanswered at the White Hart are solved once and for all.

The little alley wench

I'll tell you a story of a journalist friend of mine, who had what he described as a very strange experience – although I would say it was perfectly natural. One evening, while on an assignment in Willenhall, he was making his way toward the town centre when he mistakenly turned off up a little alley. Halfway along he found himself walking around someone who wasn't there, he just sensed that there was. In fact, he apologised out loud

The Little Ally Wench of Willenhall.
(Courtesy of Graham Walsh)

for bumping into them! Stopping to look back, he was surprised to see no one in sight. He scratched his head, blinked and walked on, stopping briefly to enquire of a gentleman direction to the street where he had parked his car. The man told him to go back down the alley and turn left. My friend asked the man if there was another way. The gent told him of a longer route, and walked away with a puzzled expression on his face.

The following day the journalist told a colleague at his West Bromwich newspaper office about the incident, who agreed to go to the alley and check it out, which he duly did; reporting back that he neither saw nor sensed anything at all. By now the time was four-thirty in the afternoon and my friend decided that he must return quickly to the alley. He did so, arriving at exactly five o'clock. Walking up the alley he came to the spot and, once more, had to move around someone or something invisible.

At that moment an elderly man from a little factory situated in the alley poked his head round the door, looked at my sturdy friend, and enquired of him, 'Psychic are you, son?'

'Err, I don't think so,' was the reply.

'Oh I see. Well, do you believe in the spirit world or ghosts?' asked the old man.

'No of course not!' the journalist answered.

'You're not the first to get stuck there, you know,' continued the old fellow. 'Oh no, not by a long shot! Shall I tell you who barred your way?'

'Please do,' answered my friend.

'Well, according to my grandmother, a woman and her young daughter lived right here in the alley, about where you were stopped. No father, but lots of uncles, if you know what I mean! Well, one evening a man called while the mother was out and he killed the little wench. When the woman returned and found her daughter, she was so broken-hearted that she killed herself by slashing her wrists with an open razor. According to my grandmother, this made her spirit earth-bound because she committed suicide. The little wench chose to stop with her mother and it's the little wench that stops psychics like you and tries to get them to help her mother.'

'That's quite a story,' said my friend. 'Look, I must write this up. When can I contact you again?'

'Well, you might see me here if you want,' answered the man, pointing to the nameplate of his factory.

The next day, the journalist told his boss what he had come across and was given the go-ahead to write a feature story. Looking in the telephone directory he found the name of the factory and rang up, asking for the old man by name. A voice on the other end of the line answered angrily, 'Is this some kind of joke? That was my grandfather's name, and he's been dead for thirty years!'

Dick Whittington and the black coach of Kinver

Yes, that's right; the legendary Lord Mayor of London did originally come from Kinver! But forget the story of the little street urchin, for that he never was! He was, in fact, the son of one William Whittington, lord and master of the village of Kinver, or Kinfare as it was then called. Richard Whittington, or plain Dick as history has labelled him, was the youngest son of William Whittington, who lost his title of Lord of Kinfare when he offended the king by marrying for the second time without His Majesty's consent. William, however, being a clever man, foresaw his lordly downfall and quickly sold the title and manor freehold to one Thomas de Lowe for a large sum of money.

This is where Dick Whittington's adventures in London were to start. His father and wife quickly set off for pastures new and Dick was made apprentice to an old family friend of his own mother's relatives, Baron Fitzwarren, a gentleman merchant of London town, who trained and treated him as though he was his own son. It is said, however, that Dick shed many tears for his beloved Kinver, to which he could not return – at least not to his former position that is.

Time and fate were to see Dick Whittington grow up into a fine gentleman who prospered exceptionally well, and position quickly came his way. Ultimately, he rose to the post of Lord Mayor of London. It should also be noted that he raised the money to refurbish and eventually rebuild St Bartholomew's Hospital, among other capital landmarks. But the rags-to-riches story of pantomime simply is not true. Dick Whittington of Kinver would certainly not have carried all his worldly possessions in a red-spotted handkerchief slung over his shoulder on a stick, and he would not have walked to London from Gloucester as the legend tells us. No, it is more likely that he made that famous journey in one of the luxurious black coaches as used by the gentry at the time.

It is said by some historians that Dick Whittington never returned to Kinver again. But it seems strange that he would not wish to see the place of his birth and boyhood, and a story claimed by locals to be true is that Dick Whittington tried to buy back the Manor of Kinver but continually failed in his efforts. He did, however, frequently return for visits. According to some, he still does, and that on heady summer nights at certain times in the

Dick Whittington and the Black Coach of Kinver. (Courtesy of Graham Walsh)

evening hours, a black coach and horses can be seen travelling up from the Whittington Inn towards the old Kidderminster road. Some locals even claim to have seen the crest of the Lord Mayor of London on the side of the coach! Perhaps there was one grain of truth in the old legend and Dick Whittington did turn again – towards Kinver village that is. It may well be that he still does today. Who knows, one of these dark, murky nights maybe he'll stop and offer you a lift to London in his black coach?

The handsome young man from the Noah's Ark

For many years the Noah's Ark pub at Tipton was kept by local boxing hero Tommy Cartwright, and his lovely wife, Milda. Tommy was scared of no one, for he had fought many hundreds of times, always a crowd-pleaser who put the other man on the defensive. One night, however, upon waking in the early hours, he found a man standing over him in what appeared to be a fighting pose. Being a professional fighter and still half asleep, Tommy thought he had taken a count in a contest. He rose, hitting out at the man, who immediately disappeared into thin air, leaving Tommy swinging punches at the empty space in front of him.

A short time after this occurrence the ghost returned, but this time he appeared to Tommy's wife, Milda. Again it was in the bedroom but, on this occasion, Tommy and Milda had their baby daughter in bed with them as she had been unwell and was being watched over by her mother between catnaps. At one moment of consciousness Milda looked down

The Noah's Ark pubic house.

at the bottom of the bed and saw a young man dressed in a smart suit in a flecked, tweed mixture, which was popular some years ago. He appeared to be looking at Milda and the baby, quite unaware of being observed himself. Milda described him as one of the most handsome young men imaginable, whose flaxen blond hair contrasted with his soulful dark-brown eyes and fair skin. He seemed to radiate complete happiness, contentment and extreme friendliness, not at all the way he had been with Tommy. She felt that he seemed to be just enjoying watching the mother and child, when he suddenly became aware of being watched too and simply vanished before them.

Some time later, Milda told a long-term customer at the pub about her experience. The man looked at her in shock, telling her that her description exactly matched the son of the previous tenant, a lad named George. 'My son's best mate, he was!'

'Was?' asked Milda.

'Oh yes me love, WAS! He passed away when he was nineteen. Died years ago, suddenly, so he did,' he answered.

Many people claim to have seen young George, and he never caused Tommy or Milda Cartwright any real trouble, apart from fancying his chances with Tommy that one night! Perhaps he just wanted to spar with the local hero, which many young men would have loved to have done at that time.

Tommy Cartwright passed away some years ago, and Milda lives nearby, and, as far as I know, George is still at the Noah's Ark in Tipton.

The Dudley Devil and the Tipton Slasher

For centuries the Black Country has been renowned for its mystics and fortune-tellers. I am told that Bilston, for instance, had a lady called Big Madge, who, around 1820, was

The author and the statue to William Perry, the Tipton Slasher.

considered an exceptionally gifted seer of the future, who used the playing cards and Tarot equally well, while Bumble Hole, Netherton, was the home of Theophillus Dunn, known as the Dudley Devil, who was also said to be gifted at telling the future of both the locals and the rich and famous from further afield.

Perhaps one of Dunn's most remarkable predictions was the downfall of one of the Black Country's most famous sons, William Perry – bare-knuckle champion prize-fighter of all England, and known as the Tipton Slasher. One of the Slasher's entourage arranged a meeting with Dunn in the early 1850s to have his fortune told (a practice as popular in the Black Country then as it is today), and, having closed his hand on Perry's half-crown, answered him in rhyme, saying:

> Slasher, yow'll stop as yow started,
> Yow'll get all yow gi'd in one goo.
> Yow and yer pub will be parted,
> Tum Little will mek it come true.

William Perry laughed and let Theophillus Dunn's prediction fade into the depths of his memory. He duly went on to smash all-comers to defeat before retiring to pulling pints in his own pub. However, in 1857, he was tempted to return to the ring to defend his title in what he considered an easy fight against Tom Sayers, a small man weighing about 11st, the Slasher by now weighing around 16st. However, he was also thirty-eight years old; ancient for a prize-fighter, even one of the greatest.

Unwisely, he sold the pub he had owned outright, all his furniture, jewellery and possessions, and backed himself with every penny he owned to win the fight with Tom Sayers. I do not wish to go into details of the contest, except to say that the title changed hands, with the Slasher taking a dreadful beating that left him a broken and penniless man with Theophillus Dunn's rhyme ringing in his ears:

> Slasher, yow'll stop as yow started,
> Yow'll get all yow gi'd in one goo.
> Yow and yer pub will be parted …

And of course, as predicted, Tom Little had made it come true!

The haunted Black Country painting

Mary Rose told me an unusual story. Around thirty years ago she bought a fairly ordinary-looking oil painting in a second-hand shop in Horseley Fields, Wolverhampton. The painting depicted a castle tower standing on a small piece of coastal land, which she felt was rather like Scotland.

She liked the painting, but back at home it unnerved her, and both her children insisted it scared them. The first night she put it up it fell off the wall twice, so she had her husband secure it with a screw and rawl-plug holding, but when they awoke the following morning it was on the floor once more. Mrs Rose's son claimed that he saw figures coming out of the tower, while his sister said there were sometimes faces on the painting that scared her. Mr Rose insisted that although there was nothing to the claims, he felt it had to go, and the painting came into my hands as a gift, to see if I could sort it out psychically, so to speak.

I thought I had, and duly sold it on to a lady, who hung it on the wall of her New Age shop on the Walsall road. Some people who came into her shop absolutely loved the painting and wanted to buy it, others didn't like it at all and said it scared them because they could see unusual ghostly figures and lights. As time went by, the painting was sold on and it even went to America at one time, amazingly to some friends of mine who insisted they wanted it, but they didn't keep it long before they sold it to a couple, who actually lived in, of all places, my home town of Willenhall. The strange thing is that everyone who has had the painting has apparently had some unusual experience with it.

Being a well-known medium, one gentleman who met me completely by chance at a psychic event asked if he could give me a present because he was scared by it. He said it was a lovely oil painting but he didn't like it and a medium had told him to give it to a medium by the name of Philip. By now I am sure you will have gathered what it was: it was the very same painting that Mrs Rose had originally bought!

I do not believe for one minute that there is anything terribly bad about the painting, and it is quite ordinary in many ways. But I don't think it is an artistic masterpiece either, and the funny thing is it wouldn't stay on my walls either. So up into the loft it went, only to be brought down fairly recently when I was about to demonstrate mediumship in a big show at the Wolverhampton Grand Theatre in September 2008, and thought I would put the painting on display alongside some other objects with a paranormal interest. But as soon as it came down from the loft there were problems. It fell over and seemed to move of its own accord, even strange sounds seemed to emanate from it.

Lending it out to photographer friends with an interest in the paranormal, and other paranormalists, it quickly came back with some strange photographs taken of it. One in particular of the tower in the painting came out with a brilliant bright light when taken in the dark, and when the photograph was blown up and we zoomed in on the light, you could clearly see a figure in the middle that looked sort of like a 1960s hippy. Zooming in a little closer and you could clearly see the face of a Viking warrior. Other photographs showed perfectly clear globes with a white spot right in the middle. Other pictures were taken that showed what looked like a Victorian figure, a Romany vargo caravan, sometimes with people, sometimes not, and ghostly figures in the clouds. Perhaps more alarming were claims that one of my friends, upon waking one morning, saw figures coming out of the tower and the painting itself, accompanied by a general feeling that wasn't very good.

With my parapsychologist's hat on, I'm sure there is an explanation, but it is certainly a strange and spooky story. With my medium's hat on, I feel the painting would have been completed by someone in their forties from Wolverhampton or Bridgnorth, but I don't really like to tune into it too much, even for me it is not comfortable.

Someone hearing the story made an outrageously generous offer to purchase the painting, but the strange thing is, I can't bring myself to sell it! I shall probably take it to some Spiritualist churches where people are not so alarmed by such things and can view it when I am demonstrating mediumship, and I shall also send the story and some photographs to serious members of the media. Perhaps I will eventually sell it on eBay, and, if it raises the ridiculous price that people seem to think it might, use the money for worthy charities or start up a healing sanctuary or something similar. It is strange how it keeps coming back to me.

Claude, the railway ghost

Wolverhampton railway station opened in 1854, but its full construction was not completed until 1855. It was converted to standard gauge in 1869 and remained pretty much the same until 1922, when the erection of a new booking office within the booking hall, together with the stationmaster's office, was built. This is said to be where a ghost in a top hat was very first seen.

The Victorian gentleman, nicknamed Claude by the station's staff, regularly puts in an appearance on the station platform, especially around the month of October, but there have also been reports of him actually travelling on the trains. Some people described his shade as being so life-like that they took him for an actor, or someone dressed up in fancy dress. One young man even claimed that Claude sat next to him for a few moments on one train journey, before standing up, lifting his hat, and dissolving into thin air. Luckily, Claude has always been described as a pleasant ghost, and has also been witnessed at Birmingham, Shrewsbury and Crewe stations at one time or another. Now a ghost that travels, that really is unusual!

Arthur Smith and Rachael Bannister told the story of Claude on their popular Birmingham Ghost Walk, and a customer care officer for Virgin Trains who attended one of the walks confirmed that many of her clients had reported seeing Claude, although apparently she had not had the pleasure (or displeasure) of seeing him herself. Some people

Wolverhampton station, where Claude has been spotted.

seem to think that Claude had links to the Wolverhampton Grand Theatre and may have been part of the management, or perhaps an actor at the wonderful old theatre, which is situated in the centre of Wolverhampton city.

After conducting some research, Smith and Bannister claim to have discovered the story of a gentleman who ended his life by taking deadly poison on a train journey. An interesting idea, but my research suggests strong links to the theatre. Other informants feel that a bomb, believed to have been planted by the IRA, which exploded in 1939, may have been the key in some way to bringing about a haunting and that Claude may be part of this scenario. But surely in 1939 a top hat would not have been the attire of gentlemen generally in and around the Wolverhampton railway station area? I believe the bomb incident is more relevant to the eerie shouts and screams that are heard late at night on occasions, especially when it is foggy or very cold on the platform. But whatever the truth is, the station certainly appears to be haunted by several ghosts or shades from the past.

Michael Pennington, the ghost who communicated by computer

A very interesting ghost story is the alleged story of Michael Pennington, a ghost who communicated stories and predictions by computer after claiming he had been clubbed to death while walking alongside the canal in Oldbury in 1971, and that his ghost haunts a derelict building close to the canal being unable to rest in peace. The story goes that a computer firm operating from the building received communication through a lady known as Janet, telling them of the story of Michael.

He is claimed to have said that he lived for number of years in a very old house in Oldbury that was in a very dilapidated state, and which used to be used as a boatyard for the canal.

He also claimed that after being beaten, he had been put down the coal shaft of the property and that he was dead. Subsequently, websites grew out of the story and even an eBay book and a possible subsequent paper copybook seems to be in the offing from this spooky tale.

Many people have researched this story but, as yet, have not found a body or a positive link to the story of his death. Whether it is an elaborate hoax or an interesting Black Country ghost story, no one can say for sure, but it looks set to run for quite some time to come.

The phantom flock of pigeons

One of the strangest cases I have ever been asked to investigate was on the Lunt council estate near Vulcan Road. A young couple had been allocated a council house there and were very excited when they visited the house after receiving the keys from a council official. Quickly moving through every room in the property, they felt it was perfect for them and decided they would take it. The couple had two small children who were pestering mum and dad to go into the garden to see what it was like. Giving into their tugs and pleading, the couple went through the back door and saw before them a very nice little garden that would be wonderful for the kids to play in.

They loved it, but couldn't understand why there was still an old garden swing and a bit of what looked like an old-fashioned, black-and-white striped shed in one corner. Suddenly, and without warning, the doors flew open of their own accord and out poured what seemed like hundreds of pigeons of all colours. The young mother knew what sort of birds

A phantom flock of pigeons has been seen in Bilston.

they were, 'They're tumblers!' she exclaimed to her husband. 'My brothers used to keep them, but they will have to go.' The couple described them as being literally everywhere, but as they went back into the house and looked out of the kitchen window, the young mum exclaimed, 'They've gone, every one of them has gone.' The couple immediately went back outside: not only was there not a pigeon to be seen, but the black and white shed and the swing had gone too!

'We're not living here, it's haunted!' said the young woman.

'Oh, there's got to be an answer to it,' replied her husband. 'Perhaps they were homing birds?'

'If they were homing birds,' she answered, 'then where's the shed gone?'

She grabbed the kids and insisted they left there and then. They handed back the keys and refused the property. They were too embarrassed to tell the councillor their experience and decided to say the property didn't suit them. Of course, this caused the couple a lot of difficulties because the council tend to put you further down the list if you refused what seemed to be a suitable property.

But who could blame them? Who would want to share their home with hundreds of birds, especially if they were from the ghost realms? The strange thing is that the people who eventually took this house never had the experience, although other residents in the area have told me the house was definitely haunted by old Jack, who had passed over many years ago, though not while living in the house, for he had been in a care home for the latter part of his life. But the tumblers were his and some people said that after he left, the birds kept returning to the house over and over again until, eventually, they all seemed to move away. And the swing? Well, apparently that had been Jack's granddaughter's at one time.

Who put Bella in the wych elm?

A murder case that shocked the Black Country and which coined the phrase, 'Who put Bella in the wych elm?' remains unsolved to this day.

Legends a-plenty have grown around the case. Some say the answer lies in espionage relevant to the Second World War, others that it came about because of her wish to end a love affair, while others claim that she was dispatched to the other world by gypsies. No one really knows for sure, but it was a horrible crime by any standards, that took place in the mid-1940s. The less-than-expert forensic investigations of those days suggested she had been suffocated with her own undergarments, her body then jammed into the tree where her remains were gradually eaten away by the wild creatures of the woods. Across the area the same words appeared on walls, 'Who put Bella in the wych elm?' Some believe there was a cryptic message in those words as to the murder of this poor girl

The body was found on 19 April 1943 by four boys from Wollescote, who were searching for bird's nests in Hagley Woods. When peering into the elm, one of the boys saw a skull grinning up at him. At first the boys thought it was an animal, but further investigation by adults and the police of course proved this was not the case, and an announcement was made to the public that the murder of a woman by suffocation had taken place. Very little was left of her remains, but within the wych elm itself was found a wedding ring and a pair of women's black shoes.

Forensic scientist Professor J.M. Webster reconstructed the skeleton in his laboratory and came to the conclusion that it was of a woman aged around thirty-five, that she had given birth to a child, was about 5ft in height, was not employed in manual work, and that her hair would have been mousy brown. She had also had a tooth removed not long before her murder. He calculated that she had been in the tree for about eighteen months. One excellent clue was that the front incisor teeth were unusually crossed over. With all this information, and a massive police hunt, people hoped the murderer would be brought to justice fairly quickly. However, this was not to be the case, and to this day the case remains unsolved and unanswered.

Many people consider the place of the wych elm to be scary and haunted. Male and female visions have been seen, and the terrible sound of screams can be most unnerving to those sensitive enough to hear them. Does the poor lady known as Bella return to this patch of woodland, perhaps searching for that wedding ring, or drawn back to the awful moment of her passing to the other world. And will the case ever be solved? No one can say for sure, but one thing that can be said for certain is that it is a mighty spooky story all round, isn't it?

The haunted fire station

The old fire station in Rolfe Street was said to be haunted by the ghost of Tommy Chandler. Mary Bodfish told me the following story about her late father, who served at Smethwick Fire Brigade between 1940 and 1967. He was a very down-to-earth individual who was never bothered about working alone in the station workshops, but there were other men who felt somewhat differently and ascribed any strange occurrences on the premises to the presence of Thomas Chandler, a former chief of the brigade.

Thomas Chandler's life was entirely bound up in the Smethwick Fire Brigade. He had joined as an auxiliary in 1879, and on the opening of Rolfe Street Fire Station in 1910, he was appointed resident captain, being promoted to chief officer a year later. A widower, he lived on the premises, but after forty-three years of service, in 1923, Smethwick Corporation had to give him notice of retirement. It seems that the prospect of being severed from all that had given meaning to his life was more than he could contemplate and shortly afterwards he was found dead in bed. The inquest heard that he had died at about 1 a.m., 'with his head swathed in bedclothes, and a piece of piping close to his mouth. This was attached to a gas bracket and the room was full of gas.' Chandler was buried with full Fire Brigade honours at the cemetery in Holly Lane. The people of Smethwick mourned the loss of the man who had served them for so long, and a public subscription fund paid for a fine copper memorial plaque, showing him with his neatly trimmed, pointed beard and wearing his brass helmet. This was erected on the wall of the fire station's engine room, giving the appearance of the former chief still watching the crews every time they raced for their equipment in response to an alarm of fire.

It was not long before some claimed the chief had not left the premises. Firemen on night duty reported hearing footsteps crossing the empty upper floor, usually around 1 a.m. Others spoke of a cold spot felt in the watch room, a tapping on the shoulder when alone, and clouds of grey mist seen hovering in various parts of the premises. More alarming was the experience of a cook, who was reading a noticeboard on the kitchen wall, only to see the board take off and hover over her head before crashing to the ground. An even odder occurrence took place when the memorial plaque was being renovated. The dovetailed joints on the frame could not be budged when it was tried to split them apart, but during the night, while the plaque remained in a locked room, the frame split into two, being found the next morning to have parted at the dovetail, with the pieces about 6in apart. Then, after the sudden death of a colleague, one fireman firmly believed that he saw the dead man in uniform walking with Chandler through the dormitory.

At times, those on duty would become very nervous of the spooky goings-on and on one occasion women in the watch room became so frightened that they even put the bells down and called out all the firemen. During the Fire Brigade strike in 1979, one man was outside on picket duty on a dark night with no one actually inside the premises. To his horror, he saw the doors of the engine house start to open by themselves – that was enough for him and he packed up and left. It must be said, however, that when I related this incident to a man who was in the brigade at Rolfe Street at the same time, he informed me that the doors were always doing that, as they had been specially weighted so that they could be released quickly and save time getting the fire engines out. Apparently, the weighting was very delicately balanced, and vibration, such as a heavy lorry passing by, could tip them!

In 1979, Rolfe Street fire station was closed after new premises were opened in Stoney Lane, but you can still see the memorial plaque to Thomas Chandler, where it was re-erected on the wall of the new engine room. The old premises were put to other uses, including, for a time, workshops and offices for the National Association for the Care and Resettlement of Offenders. A few years ago I happened to be introduced to a woman who worked there, and got talking to her about my memories of the old fire station. She told me that she occasionally had to sleep on the premises and one night she had awakened to see the figure of a man in the room, looking at her. To my astonishment, she described him as being in his sixties and having a neatly trimmed, pointed beard. He was not a frightening figure, in fact he was chuckling merrily to himself and she drifted back to sleep again. This lady had never heard of Tommy Chandler until I told her of him and to this day we wonder if he paid her a call while doing the rounds of the fire station that had been the world he knew and loved.

The Dudley tunnels

Tours around these famous tunnels are popular with people from all over the country, and several visitors have reported strange experiences and seeing ghosts, and some of the boats themselves have been unexplainably pulled in another direction, as if by unseen hands. One such boat, the *Electra*, had just this experience some years ago.

Legend has it that two children on a home-made raft tried to travel the Wren's Nest Tunnel, but it had overturned in the water and both children were drowned in the murky depths. People have reported seeing a woman crying and wringing her hands in the Shirts Mill Tunnel. Some paranormal groups feel this is the ghost of a lady who cries for her husband, George, a miner who lost his life in the days when Dudley was a mining Mecca. Shirts Mill Basin is also nicknamed Murder Mine, and is believed to have been the site of such a crime. It is possible, because, in 1950, whilst work was being undertaken in this area, the skeleton of a young woman was discovered.

It is not unusual for the lights carried by individuals or on the barges to inexplicably go out, particularly in an area known as the dark cavern, which also has a reputation for being 'chillingly cold as the grave'. One of the most famous caves is the Singing Cavern, where many people are believed to have lost their lives while digging for coal. Several reports have been made of the sound of voices apparently singing songs, quite apt for a cave called the Singing Cavern, and many barge skippers have also heard voices and unexplained noises there too. There is also reported the sound of someone playing a Jew's harp, and on other occasions a harmonica.

Other reports include unusual orbs that have been photographed, and strange balls of glowing gold light that seem to pass along the tunnels. These have been viewed by several people and are thought to be the energy of spirit beings, which is possible, but we also have to consider the possibility of ball lightning. These waterways of Dudley can certainly be very spooky at times.

A hauntingly agricultural site

Northicote Farm was probably built in the very early 1600s, and we know that in the seventeenth century it was owned and lived in by the Underhill family. Ownership later transferred to the Whitgreaves and was probably closely linked to Moseley Court. Northicote Farm was probably looked after and tended by local agricultural labourers under the supervision of tenant farmers. Legend has it that King Charles II, fleeing from Cromwell's Roundheads after defeat at the Battle of Worcester, called at the farm and asked for assistance, but was turned down, leading the king to move quickly to Boscobel House and the famous story of hiding in a tree that is part of English history. Could this be the reason why staff at the farm have reported heavy banging on the doors from unseen hands

An artist's impression of the Northicote Lady.

or why an elderly lady is seen wringing her hands and holding her head? Was she sorry for refusing the king entry, or did he find some vengeance when put back on the throne?

Another lady who is seen wearing clothes that would probably be associated to the time of the Civil War, is said to give an energy described as being pleasant and calming, and the picture above, a likeness provided by a local artist, is said to be very similar to how she appears to those lucky enough to see her.

There is another story of a man described as an agricultural labourer, who also holds his head, apparently, as legend has it, still searching for a love that vanished around the building in those far off days. The Blue Room is always described as having a strange feeling, even scary or eerie on occasions. People have described the feeling of fainting or passing out, or of spider's web-type sensations coming across their face. Footsteps are regularly heard on the staircase that leads to the upper floor, together with stories of the lady with a sweeping brush or broom who sweeps the floor and is visible to some in the restaurant area, with reports that on occasions she suddenly runs from the room.

Ladies have reported feeling uneasy on visiting the toilets in the area close to the upstairs restaurant, and some women have seen the appearance of a woman in Victorian-style clothing and a man in a top hat, who, one correspondent said, cheekily doffed his hat to her before dissolving back into the ether! The stable block is also claimed to be an unusual place where, on occasion, figures looking like farm labourers and others wearing attire of a more aristocratic nature have all been seen. Within the grounds itself there have been many reports of figures that appear then suddenly disappear in the night, and a laughing cavalier and two very dour Roundheads have also been seen. Northicote Farm is a great place to visit, particularly for the wonderful events they organise at Christmas and on Bonfire Night. It is also a fascinating place for those interested in ghosts and things that go bump in the night.

William Howe, the Black Country highwayman

In the Gibbet Lane area is the ghost of a horseless highwayman, guilty in his lifetime of the most awful crime of murder. Gibbet Lane links Stourbridge and Kinver, and a track there has been used by locals for centuries. My own family, who lived in Kinver and Compton, spoke of strange sounds and visions here, and it is no wonder, for on this site, or close by, murderers were hung in chains and left to rot as a deterrence to others considering a life of crime.

But it is also where Black Country highwayman, William Howe, ambushed and shot local farmer Benjamin Robins in 1812. It was market day and Benjamin, whom some members of my family believe was a distant cousin, was making his way from the market carrying a large amount of money from the sheep and other commodities he had sold that day. He had stopped off at the Nag's Head Inn before continuing to walk home to his farm in the Dunsley area, where the attack took place. Badly wounded, Benjamin staggered home and lasted ten days before dying just after Christmas 1812, but not before he had given a full description of Howe, the highwayman.

Howe fled to London, but was eventually captured and brought to trial following imprisonment at Stafford gaol, where he was hung by the neck until dead. However, Stourbridge magistrates insisted on being given the body, which was hung in chains near the spot where the crime took place in Gibbet Lane. The corpse swung for a long while until only a skeleton remained, which, according to legend, was stolen for some morbid use or

The horseless highwayman.
(Courtesy of Graham Walsh)

perhaps by some medical person requiring such an item. But legend has it that the spirit of William Howe remains trapped in the area of Gibbet Lane, frightening those that pass by.

Other legends claim that Howe's skeleton was eventually buried nearby, following some sort of ceremony by local people, though no evidence can be found to prove this. However, in 1908 a skeleton *was* found nearby, together with a rusty dagger protruding from its ribcage and, as you may have guessed, the site was close to the original gibbet tree. It is a quite amazing story, and as the saying goes, crime doesn't pay in the end, does it? It certainly didn't for William Howe, the Black Country highwayman.

The haunted nightclub

The Atlantis nightclub (now known as the Oceana) in Wolverhampton experienced a very strange haunting. The manager, Andy Millichamp, contacted the *Express & Star* and asked me – as the paper's resident expert on the paranormal – if I would visit the club to investigate a most unusual ghost story. Members of the club believed they were being haunted by, if not Elvis Presley himself, then someone whose singing voice sounded very like his.

The building had at one time been the Savoy Cinema, built in 1936, and in earlier times had been a library. The cinema was a popular place for many people, and when it was turned into the Atlantis in 1995 it continued to attract a lot of young people. The staff there told me that on occasions they could hear someone singing in the cellar in a rock'n'roll, Elvis-type manner. However, other members of staff spoke of someone laughing in a most

The entrance to the Oceana nightclub.

unpleasant way and doors that opened and slammed shut of their own accord. Another member of staff told me that rather than sinister laughter, she often heard the sound of youngsters giggling. Other instances have included glasses being thrown without human hands assisting their travel, or simply shattering for no apparent reason.

As a professional medium, my feelings were that the situations experienced were relevant to when the building had been a cinema, possibly during its time as an ABC venue, and I felt that in the top-floor area someone had committed suicide by hanging or jumping to their death. The singing and laughter I felt was just shades of yesteryear where teenagers were having fun. I was subsequently contacted by another correspondent, John, who gave me a great deal of information that suggested someone had actually committed suicide in the way I felt, and that during his time working in the building there were already a great deal of ghostly goings-on. It would seem without a shadow of a doubt that this is one of the most haunted buildings in the town.

Ladies and gentlemen, Elvis Presley has not left the building!

I am one of the presenters at Wolverhampton City Radio (WCR), and while broadcasting there one evening both myself and my producer, Jason, had a very unusual experience. That night, as part of my Fifties and Sixties Show, we were interviewing Sonny West, who had been the bodyguard and personal friend of Elvis Presley. A phone call had been made to Sonny, and the interview was conducted in this way.

The author at the Wolverhampton City Radio studios.

I went into the studio to talk to one of the presenters where a female assistant was sitting at his side, when a very loud bang suddenly happened right beside her. Both the presenter and myself looked at her but she had not been aware of the noise and had heard nothing at all. A few minutes later I took over as presenter in the studio, with my producer operating the desk opposite. As I spoke to Sonny West, I saw a bright white light at my side. As an experienced medium, this sort of thing doesn't worry me at all, and I thought I would just let it go, but after the interview had finished, Jason told me that he had seen the faint vision of a man in a white suit. It would be fair to say that Jason comes from a scientific background and doesn't believe in such things, but I think he was more than a little shocked by his experience. Did the king of rock'n'roll join us for a moment as I spoke to his old friend Sonny West and played a few of his songs? Who knows? But something strange certainly happened that night, and others at WCR have been witness to unusual experiences in the studios and other rooms at the radio station.

At one time the WCR studios had been situated in the old BBC radio studios in Queen Street, Wolverhampton. Des, who had been a presenter there at one time, told me of some very unusual spectres that seemed to flash by, and of unexplainable noises that would come from the top-floor studio, that were more discernable at around nine or ten o'clock in the evening.

The spook in riding breeches

I first became aware of the haunting stories of the Olde White Rose pub in Bilston many years ago, when members of my family told me what a strange place it was. I became quite convinced of it being haunted when I visited the building, and when a story appeared in the *Express & Star* that told of strange goings-on there. I chose this pub to be part of a haunted film series that was produced for video, and it was while filming an interview with the landlord, John Denston, that it became quite clear to me this was indeed one of the strangest buildings in the town.

Mr Denston told me that on one occasion, whilst moving beer barrels in the cellar, he was shocked to see a pair of trousered legs walking down a slope to where he was working. He left the area rather quickly, but then decided to return, armed with a large stick, believing it was an intruder. However, there before him stood a character, clearly from another world, who held out his hands to him. Mr Denston now recognised the trousers as riding breeches. The man also wore a dark tunic, was of swarthy complexion, and had long black hair. Obviously shaken, Mr Denson froze on the spot, but just as quickly as he had appeared, the figure turned and disappeared.

The building is old, possibly from the sixteenth century, and probably part of what would at one time have been a coaching inn. Many other spectres have been seen there: the chef told me of regularly seeing entities he would describe as not of this world, filtering in and out of the building, and the staff describe the cellars as particularly scary.

During our filming there, my team and I had lots of unusual experiences. On one occasion, having returned to the studio for editing, the film had inexplicably been wiped clear of all visual references. However, the sound of voices shouting as though in a temper could clearly be heard. A heavy camera on a tripod fell over of its own accord, and professional lighting kits switched themselves on and off with no assistance from the camera crew or anyone else visible. Perhaps most alarming of all was an ice-cold blast of air that made a whooshing

The Olde White Rose, Bilston.

The staircase at the
Olde White Rose.

sound as it came down the stairs and into the cellar. Again, as a professional psychic and medium, I found it rather interesting and very cooling on what had been a very hot day. The rest of the crew, however, did not share this view I can assure you!

Spooks among the ironing boards

Several people have reported strange goings-on at the Beldray Buildings, but perhaps one of the best stories I have heard was related to me by Bjorn Ben. Bjorn had worked there as a security guard and told me he heard strange knocks, bangs, and other noises that just could not be explained at around ten or eleven o'clock at night. The building was always quiet until about this time, but then all kinds of disturbances would start to happen.

Upon investigating the building, the guards found that on several occasions a radio in one of the rooms would switch itself on. On another occasion, Bjorn and a colleague had just arrived at the factory when the latter accidentally tore his trousers on a sharp piece of metal that was sticking out, and as there were sewing machines in the upstairs rooms (the company made ironing boards amongst other household appliances), the men decided they would try to repair the trousers on one of the machines.

As they were going up the stairs, their supervisor appeared, asking why the alarms were going off. The two security guards said it was impossible, as they had been switched off. Bjorn knows they had not forgotten to do this, as it was a routine procedure they had to carry out on arrival at the building, and to this day cannot explain how the alarms could have been activated.

On another occasion, the guards came upon one of the large sealed containers that had been delivered to the site by lorry. It had been positioned against the wall so that no one could possibly have got inside it, but both men could hear footsteps and someone moving about inside the container, but investigation proved that no one was.

Perhaps one of the scariest occurrences happened to Bjorn when he walked past a room that contained machines with pressurised air hoses attached to them. The machines had been switched off for a couple of days, but he could hear a loud hissing noise coming from inside the room. When he went in to investigate, he found three of the air hoses were disconnected from the machines with no explanation of how this could have happened.

Several other people have also told me about seeing shadowy figures and hearing unusual noises while they worked there. All this evidence seems to suggest there must have been some spooks among the ironing boards and ghosts in the machinery at this factory.

The motorcycle that kick-started itself into life

Rob told me a very interesting story about his grandfather's old BSA motorcycle. For many years the bike had been stored at the back of his father's garage until Rob decided to see if it would still run.

After cleaning the old machine down with paraffin and freeing off all the wheels and other moving parts with releasing spray, the day arrived when Rob drove the kick-start down on the old machine. It immediately spluttered and turned over and on the fourth kick roared into life. Rob was very pleased with himself, and thought he would see if it would be possible to get the machine MOT-tested, insured and whether it still had a relevant number plate at the DVLA Swansea Registration Office.

But the machine was to prove very strange, to quote Rob's words. One afternoon he could clearly hear the bike running in the garage. Rushing down to the garage, which was

A BSA motorcycle similar to Rob's grandfather's.

situated at the bottom of the garden, he found the machine quite silent. Walking back up to the house, again he could hear the bike running. Returning to the garage, it was silent once more. Rob didn't think any more of it, and decided not to tell his mother because it had been her father's motorcycle and it may have upset her.

Feeling strangely uneasy, he decided that the bike should go to the back of the garage again for the time being. Two or three months passed by without any further thought of it, until one day, while at work, Rob received a call on his mobile phone from his mother, asking why he had left the bike running in the garage that morning? She couldn't get into the garage and didn't know how to switch it off anyway. Rob went straight home and, once more, he found the bike silent and cold. Was it his granddad saying he wanted it to be used? Or was the machine haunted in some other way?

Whatever the reason, Rob decided to sell the bike to his uncle, who has had absolutely no problems with it at all. Apparently, it now only runs when it is kick-started, and is much admired by all and sundry at many classic motorcycle events.

The ghostly bride at the Prince of Wales

The Prince of Wales public house on the Walsall road has a quite incredible ghost story. My friend, Tara Sinclair, lived there for many years and told me the pub was definitely haunted, and that she had had personal experiences herself. When Tara was only five years old, she saw three figures walking down the passageway of the pub; a bride, with two men standing either side of her in morning suits. Tara remembered they seemed to be higher than the floor at that time, as if they were walking on another level.

Some years later, a customer who came into the pub, which was owned by her father, and told him that at one time a woman had committed suicide in the cellar there. She had been due to get married but was jilted, so the story goes, because she had been having an affair with another man. The passage is very spooky and leads on the one side to St Giles' Church and what was at one time the youth club on the opposite side of the road.

Tara and her family believe that the lady who haunted the cellar and walked the corridors were one and the same person. Tara's father would always know when she was about because there would be a sudden drop in temperature – a very real one at that – because it would cause the beer to fob (a term in publican's language for beer going very frothy). Tara's dad, a down-to-earth man, would openly tell the ghost to leave the area as he was trying to run a business. Amazingly, the communication must have worked because the ghost would leave, the temperature would rise, and the beer would return to its required normal condition, meaning everyone, customers and staff alike, were happy.

The family had a dog called Vimto who didn't like to go in the cellar however much he was coaxed, and, when he did, would stare at something unseen to humans, bare his teeth and his hackles would rise. Another ghost seen in this area was a puppy, which could quite clearly see you as well, and would interact by running towards you but fading away before it reached you.

There were also ghosts in the lounge of the pub – a part of the building Tara never liked. Being sensitive, she felt she knew where the problem was. There was a false wall in the room and, in her words, she would never go either side of the wall if she could help it. Even when playing in the yard close by, she felt it was somewhere best to avoid. She never actually saw anything in there but knew something strange abounded. An addition followed when Tara was discussing this story with her father recently. He told her his friend, Bobby Smith, had been in the pub reading cards psychically. He was always uncannily accurate when he did this, and had advised Tara's father that there was something really bad in the lounge, but that the bad spirit was kept in equilibrium and balance by a good spirit.

On another occasion Tara's friend, Dawn, was visiting the pub one day when they were both in junior school together. Later, Dawn asked Tara whom the old lady dressed in the old-fashioned, high-necked dress, standing at one of the windows, was? She wondered who would wear such weird clothes.

I have long come to the conclusion that Willenhall is the most haunted town in the Black Country, and possibly one of the most haunted places in the whole of the UK. Certainly the Prince of Wales, its passages, cellars and other areas, have an incredible tale or three to tell, and it is good when you can get first-hand accounts – such as that provided by Tara and her family.

The man who came back to life

A man who has lived in Wolverhampton for many years told me of a most fascinating story that happened when his father was a boy in his village in India. Within the village were two families with the same surname but whom were unrelated, and within these two families were two men who also had the same first name. One of the men throughout his life suffered from illness, and had for many years been teetering on the brink of death; the other was in perfect health.

One day, completely without warning, the healthy man passed away and a funeral was arranged by his grieving family. At the funeral, while everyone was quietly mourning the man, some members of the family noticed that the fingers of his hand were twitching slightly, gradually moving more so, until he was able to sit up. As you can imagine, the family rejoiced at the fact that he was alive and well, even if they were as equally shocked as they were overjoyed.

The man told his family he had visited the higher life, or rather had been taken there by two warriors, one either side of him, who led him to a desk surrounded either side by piles of books, and 'manned' by an elderly gentleman with a long grey beard. The bearded man asked the man his name, to which he replied honestly. The elderly gent looked at him, then chastised the two warriors, saying there had been a terrible mistake and that, although the man in front of him was who he said he was, he was not the right person and that the two warriors were to return him immediately. Apparently, they had been sent to bring a man of his name to the higher life, but he was not the one they should have brought back.

Acting upon the request, the warriors took the man between them and led him to a room that had a wall with a tiny hole in it no bigger than a coin from which light seemed to enter. They pushed him into this hole, his 'body' somehow passing through it, and the next thing the man knew he was lying amidst his friends and family, his garments those of the deceased, though he was very much alive and well, if a little confused!

A few days after the man's miraculous return to the living, his family were advised that there had been another passing in the village, this time of the other man with the same name. This person, however, did not return to life. It would seem that at times even those in the heavens get it wrong, and sometimes changes have to be made to fulfil each and everyone's passage from this world into the next. This is an incredible story which I am assured is the absolute truth.

PART TWO

AN A–Z OF SHORTER GHOST STORIES FROM THE BLACK COUNTRY

Aldridge

There is an interesting story of a young couple keen to purchase a rather nice house in Whetstone Lane in this particular area. However, whilst viewing the property, the couple's child insisted to his parents that he did not wish to live there under any circumstances and that it had a horrible feel to it. Recent research suggests that a very bad fire happened in the vicinity of the house. Is this what made the young boy fearful of living there, and did he have a natural sensitivity that perhaps his parents did not?

Barr Beacon

In the distant past, Barr Beacon was said to be a hill used for Druid sacrifices. In recent years, witnesses claim to have seen a very strange procession of druid-like people slowly passing by in single file. It is also a place where one of my correspondents, Jay, was quite sure he saw his friend, who had passed away a few days before, about 50yds away from him on the hills as he was walking with his dog.

Normal or Paranormal?

One example of this type of occurrence could be something a friend of mine described as the 'Matrix Experience': that is, after leaving this world, or being dead if you like, an etheric image of the body carries on and can still be seen for a short while after. Then again, perhaps Jay witnessed a sort of hypnotic experience of wishing to see his friend and his mind gave him the opportunity to see him for a moment or two.

Bearwood

Warley Park is situated in Abbey Road, on the very edge of the Black Country. At one time Warley Abbey stood here, before it was demolished in 1968 by the council. The abbey is linked to Halesowen Abbey, and legend has it that some of the abbey stones may have been part of the secondary building in Warley Park. The abbey was built by Hubert Galton, who came from a Quaker family and who inherited great wealth on his mother's side from the people who built up the banking business of Barclays. The abbey and park are said to be haunted by the Grey Lady, who is either seen walking in and around the grounds or more regularly in the car park area close to the woods. Legend has it that the Grey Lady was a member of the Galton family, and was murdered. Other stories suggest that she may have committed suicide through a love affair which was cause and brought about her sad demise. There is also a report of an oriental gentleman, and a little black boy that apparently runs across your pathway. Perhaps both are the shades of former servants of the wealthy Galton family?

The Grey Lady of Warley Park.
(Courtesy of Graham Walsh)

Bentley

Andrew Perrins tells a very interesting story of the Pouk, or Puck, in his book, *Ghosts and the Folklore Around Barr Beacon*. This mischievous and malicious goblin could take on the guise of a very ugly and hideous dwarf in possession of a horse's head and cloven feet of a goat, who would lie in wait to scare unsuspecting wayfarers as they passed by. Of course, in those days Bentley was a large, lonely common, not dominated by the council estates of today, and the Pouk belonged to those times apparently.

It is certainly something you wouldn't like to meet as you make your way up Churchill Lane today, is it?

Normal or Paranormal?

It may be hard to believe, but some crypto-zoologists who research and search for the existence of very rare animals, have come to the conclusion that some creatures may be what is termed as 'out of place animals'; ghosts and apparitions, or shape-shifters; human or animal ghosts that have taken on the shape of other creatures. Could this fit in with the case of the Pouk? On the other hand it could be one of those urban myths that has done the circuits and caused those with a vivid imagination to believe they have seen or experienced what would certainly be a very scary occurrence.

An artist's impression of what the Pouk might have looked like.
(Courtesy of Graham Walsh)

The Cavalier's Rails, Bentley.

Bentley

There has long been told the story of Bentley's Laughing Cavalier, usually reported to be seen on the hill close to the church, sometimes appearing to be looking out, at other times walking across the small parkway in that area. A few years ago, there was a report from a young couple who said that as they stood by the railings around the monument on the top of the hill, they heard a hideous eerie laugh behind them and, turning round, saw the cavalier, this time on horseback amidst an unusual mist that faded into nothing.

Bilston

There have been many very reliable reports of the ghost of a woman dressed in a long black frock and bonnet and carrying a glowing lantern. She is said to appear fairly frequently in the area of Turles Hill, and it would appear to be a long-standing haunting.

Woman in a black frock and bonnet. (Courtesy of Graham Walsh)

Bilston

Gibbet Lane was once an area renowned for its patronage and association with local criminals, which is surprising really, considering many convicts had been gibbeted at the nearby bridge and left to hang until the wild creatures had had their pick at the remains. No wonder then that many people have reported seeing spectres of ghosts in this area, often in capes or work clothes of yesteryear.

Bilston

The Old Meeting Road at Coseley is said to be haunted by the ghost of an old miner known as Tall John, who frequently makes his way at early morn and evening fall to some long-since lost and forgotten mine. Susan Taylor, who wrote to me some years ago, actually claimed she had spoken to the ghost of Tall John, who lifted his cap to her and spoke in broad Black Country brogue, 'Good mornin'ter thee, missus.' Susan assured me she did answer back with a curt, 'Good morning,' before leaving the area just as quickly as her feet would carry her!

Bilston

The Coseley Youth Centre in Old Meeting Road is reputedly haunted by the former caretaker, who has been seen checking windows and doors, just as dedicated and, at times, as noisily as he had been in his life-form! If the reports are true, this would be a perfect example of a spirit who would appear not to know that he has passed over.

Coseley Youth Centre.

Bilston

There is a legend that suggests a black cat that runs across the road where Lidl is situated is not of this world, yet may warn people of dangerous driving or speeding cars. It is an unusual story, but more than one Bilstonian has told me of this tale, so perhaps this is indeed a lucky black cat, full of good spirit and intentions for humans.

The Black Cat of Bilston. (Courtesy of Graham Walsh)

Bilston

Jenny told me a quite amazing story of a haunted brush, of all things! She and her partner sell second-hand goods on the local markets and would often clear houses where people had passed away and their families had sold off the contents of their homes quite cheaply. One particular house clearance had a most unusual experience. While working with her partner loading their van with commodities from a house in Coseley, one of the rooms they cleared had quite a lot of rubbish and other bits and bobs on the wooden floor. Jenny said to her partner, 'When you've taken the last couple of boxes out, leave that brush in the corner and I'll sweep up.' He went to the van and she went into another room. Walking back into the previous room, she found it was spotless and the brush was in the opposite corner. 'Have you swept up?' she asked her partner. He was emphatic that it was not him, and replied, 'You said you were going to do it.'

'Well, I don't know what's going on then, because I haven't either,' she told him.

They both came to the conclusion that it could only have been ghostly hands that pushed the brush, as absolutely no one else was there at the time. The pair quickly completed the clearance, locked the premises, and left the brush behind! All I can say is that someone like myself, who doesn't find such things scary, would have been only too delighted to have such a brush around! Jenny definitely was not though.

Bilston

There are pools and canals situated in this area where several people have had the same experience of seeing the headlights of a car that sinks into the dark, murky waters of the pools and nearby canal, or 'the cut' as it is often referred to by the locals of the area, and of a similar vehicle that comes up the lane itself at great speed with full headlights ablaze. Mr Turner reported seeing the vehicle, which he described as looking like an old-fashioned Vanguard-type car, that he had to swerve to avoid. The car itself seemed to career to its left and vanish from sight. Again, this could be a replay of an accident or near-accident that has imprinted its memory into the ether and plays back as if being seen on film or through a video recorder. One individual also reported hearing screams and a very loud bang, but saw nothing at all. This may have been an audio version of this strange haunting.

Bilston

Some of my friends of Romany descent tell me of the strange vision of a Romany vargo that some people could see quite clearly in the area that has now built up around Vulcan Road. Not only was there a vision of a caravan, but of a campfire and family too. Romany people have always been known to have second-sight, and to be naturally attuned to nature, and the two girls who saw this vision are both of Romany stock, but were brought up in homes in and around Bilston. But is there something within them that helped them perhaps see visions of their ancestors from times gone by? As they have grown into mature women, they still insist that what they saw was very real to them. Similar visions have also been seen around Bentley, Walsall and, perhaps not so unusually, in the Gipsy Lane area of Willenhall. Perhaps the name itself is rooted to an historical link in some way. Others claim that in Willenhall and Bilston, the ghosts of Petilengro and Bostock, both gypsies, put in appearances, but are only ever seen by those that have the blood of the Rom within their veins.

Some of my friends of Romany descent
claim strange visions are seen here.
(Courtesy of Graham Walsh)

Bilston

The Trumpet is quite famous for being visited by musicians from far and wide, and many of the local pop groups in the past considered it to be 'their pub', to coin a phrase. People who worked there and visited it in the past often speak of hearing strange noises and smelling an unexplained aroma, a little like a lady's perfume. Perhaps one of the strangest ghost stories happened at the rear of the pub one Christmas Eve, where two lads saw what they described as a very attractive lady in a fur coat who stopped to speak to them, but then immediately dissolved before their very eyes. Could she have been a spooky lady of the night?

Rear of the
Trumpet in Bilston.

The Greyhound & Punchbowl Inn, Bilston.

Bilston

The Greyhound & Punchbowl Inn is one of the town's oldest pubs, so it is not surprising it has numerous alleged ghosts. Alongside the old gentleman and serving wench that have been seen, is the strange story of a couple who were having a meal there one day and got into conversation with a woman who joined them at the table. Making enquiries later of who she was, no one seemed to know, and no one had seen them talking to her either. Did the young couple talk to a ghost that day? It's a possibility, isn't it?

Black Heath

The Malt Shovel in Black Heath, situated on the High Street, is said to have an unusual ghost who used to turn the beer off at the most inconvenient of times. Doors would slowly open and then slam shut, and at one time one of the bar staff reported a bottle of rum disappearing from the cellar only to be found later in another part of the building unopened. Perhaps this ghost was attracted to spirits of a different kind!

Bloxwich

The Royal Exchange is said to be haunted by a former landlord, and some correspondents say he is particularly sensed around the building in very hot weather. According to one former regular, a strange sweaty odour can sometimes be smelt coming from behind you on occasions.

Bloxwich

Hill's House Farm is said to have a very unusual haunting that involves the noise of footsteps that sound like someone wearing slippers walking across carpet, when sudden unexplained loud cracking noises are heard. Shadowy figures also pass straight through the living room window and the noise of a car engine or some other vehicle pulls up outside on the driveway, but when you look for it no vehicle can be seen.

Brierley Hill

Almost into Stourbridge, this old traditional Black Country town has a public house known as the Starving Rascal that is so haunted by a tramp who died on the steps after being refused food, that they renamed the old place after him. They also get wet footprints that just won't go away, and other ghosts a-plenty! A former landlord, Phil Nichols, claimed it was the most haunted pub in the Midlands, and the present owners also say regulars have what can only be described as many interesting and spooky tales of ghostly goings-on to tell.

Brownhills

Brownhills is an old mining village, so it is not surprising that many people have seen what they describe as miners on their way to work, usually around six o'clock in the morning or just as dawn is breaking, but they are not of this world and are shades of another time. The village also has stories of a black and white cat, which, if seen when you are not in the best of health, allegedly brings healing your way, whereas if you should see the large black dog in the early hours of the morning, some would consider you less than fortunate. My correspondent, John, insisted it certainly seemed to bring him a poor run of bad luck after his vision of it in 2007.

The black dog of Brownhills. (Courtesy of Graham Walsh)

Brownhills

Another correspondent told me he saw the ghosts of boy scouts in Clayhanger Lane, appearing dishevelled and upset about something. There is a local legend that at one time a young lad jumped from a nearby bridge dressed in an old Bayden Powell-type scout outfit. Could this have created a playback of the situation in present times? Certainly the other boy scouts would have been alarmed and upset by such an action if they had been present.

Artist's impression of the boy scout leaping from the bridge. (Courtesy of Graham Walsh)

Brownhills

A recent story I have been told is of the ghost of a young woman who has been seen in and around the area of the open market, apparently quite unaware of being viewed. It is an unusual occurrence, as the woman, who is described as being between twenty-five and thirty, seems to suddenly stop, raise her hand, then put her finger to her lips in a manner suggesting that she is trying to hush someone unseen by the living. Some people also say that the woman wears a long coat and a red beret possibly from the 1970s.

Cannock

Hawks Green Lane is where several people have reported hearing the sound of horses' hooves and of riders shouting to one another, sometimes in the road and at other times in a nearby field. In that same field there have been some unusual reports of bright glowing lights, either gold or silver, that seem to travel from one corner of the field to the other. A friend of mine who used to ride horses there, told me that on one occasion her horse stopped dead as a golden light crossed within a few inches of his nose.

Normal or Paranormal?

Many people believe that such balls of light are spirits and that collections of them are where several spirits are gathered together. It could be that this was the spirit or ghost of another time that passed before the rider and horse. But there is another theory that such lights are something called ball lightning. Scientists and meteorologists say similar examples are seen when small pockets of gas rise from the earth caused by the movement of soil or rocks underground. This can cause electro-magnetic pockets of gas that look like lights. Much mining and tunnelling has taken place in Cannock in the past – could this be the answer to these strange occurrences?

Compton, nr Wolverhampton

There is a large house in Compton Road West that was once a nursing home. Tim, a present resident, although never having seen anything, told me of footsteps and things being moved about that sound like quite heavy objects. Tim says he hears these noises on the second floor, when he is on the floor below, especially at night. Investigations have always proved that there was neither a physical presence nor anything else that may have been the cause of the sounds. He can only assume that it is something from another time that he can hear so clearly.

Cosford

An RF398 Bomber aeroplane at the RAF Museum is said to be haunted by the ghost of a former Spitfire pilot, or an engineer who committed suicide nearby in around 1940. There are too many of these reports to be disregarded. In very recent times, I have also been told of the sound of a pistol being fired that cannot be accounted for or explained. Although Cosford is just outside the Black Country area, it is worth listing for the amazing stories which have been regularly reported in West Midlands newspapers, such as the *Wolverhampton Express & Star*, like the time two mechanics were renovating the aircraft. One of the men claimed a mysterious figure approached them, but, as he got close to the plane, he turned and disappeared. It could not have been his fellow mechanic for he was working directly in front of him. Other people at the museum have seen a man dressed as a fighter pilot; others have seen such a person in the cockpit in a leather helmet and goggles.

Objects regularly move round the museum of their own accord, and temperatures suddenly and inexplicably drop. The ghost or spirit of the pilot was even seen by a member of the camera crew who were filming there for part of the ITV series, *Wish You Were Here?* Some researchers have reported recording sounds and voices from the empty Lincoln Bomber.

Cosford has also been the site of UFO-type sightings, and two young airmen even reported a UFO landing at the nearby Cosford Barracks. It is the Aerospace Museum itself though that seems to get the most reports of unexplained phenomena.

Normal or Paranormal?

It could well be that the museum is haunted by ghosts or spirits, but there is also another possibility which is called the Stone Tape Theory. This is the situation where visual and audio recordings from the past are viewable by some people, known as sensitives, through as yet unknown or unproven stimuli. Those who believe in this theory also know it as the Holographic Universe Theory.

Darlaston

Female residents at the vicarage in Darlaston Green were allegedly woken up during the night by someone who looked very much like a vicar, smartly dressed and with a pipe in his hand or mouth. Some people speak of hearing a man singing or quoting the psalms, and he is always described as a pleasant soul or spirit.

Darlaston

In Owen Road, close to the entrance of the old Rubery Owen factory, Mick Blakemore told me of seeing the ghost of a young girl with long blonde hair, dressed in a white, flowing dress, crossing from one side of the road to the other. She has been seen on numerous occasions, sometimes stopping to smile at an individual before vanishing in front of his or her eyes. Several people actually wrote to the local newspaper claiming to have seen this girl at about 8.30 a.m. in the morning. Could she have been on her way to work at one of the nearby factories? Other people have also seen a girl of about seventeen or eighteen, who runs across this road but vanishes halfway across. She has been described as wearing a mini-skirt, long boots and with short-cropped hair, so I don't think they could be the same person. Perhaps this spot is a place that collects memories and replays them to those who are sensitive enough to see them and are there just at the right time to witness them.

Darlaston

St Leonard's churchyard has a very distinguished statue of a lady and child. Reports have been made that the child has become physical and walks away from the statue. People have also claimed to have seen stones that glow at night, strange vapours, and what has been described as a figure dressed like a monk but in a white habit, in and around the churchyard. Interestingly, I was once given a report by someone who claimed to have seen the statue move whilst in the company of five other people. It is always interesting when others can collaborate a story and have had the same experience at the same time.

Normal or Paranormal?

It is a fascinating story and it could be that some strange energy makes the statue move. But a view presented by some psychologists and parapsychologists says that if you look at something that is still for long enough, your eyes will suggest that it moves. Another view

The author with the statue of a lady and child at St Leonard's churchyard, Darlaston.

is that sometimes, if one person sees something, auto-suggestion or mass hypnosis may take place, whereby others present believe they see the same thing.

Darlaston

Jenny and Sue had a quite frightening experience whilst playing with a Ouija Board in the park. It had become something of a fascination for a group of teenage girls who would meet on Saturday afternoons and play with the board, despite being advised against such actions by others. One day, while Jenny and Sue were operating the board in the park, Sue looked up and saw a figure she described as perhaps 7ft tall and enveloped in a black mist. Jenny didn't see the figure, but as Sue ran in terror, the other girl followed, leaving the board behind. It may have been just their imagination, but they never collected the board or played with one again. Personally, I would advise everyone not to play with such things, as they can be dangerous in the wrong hands.

Ouija Board.

JB's Discotheque, Dudley.

Dudley

JB's Discotheque, which is situated at the rear of Evans's Garage in King Street, is said to have been built on the site of an old burial ground, and many of the visitors to this popular nightspot have reported strange noises. Also, on more than one occasion, reports have been made of the ghost of a young man dressed in Army uniform appearing clearly to people lucky enough to see him, or unlucky as the case may be, if you are nervous of such things!

Dudley

The Old Priory public house, opposite the police station, is alleged to be suffering a poltergeist-type haunting. It is also said to be haunted by several other ghosts as well. One character, known as Old Smokin' Joe, is known to be around because of the smell of very heavy tobacco in the air. Another vision of a girl known simply as the serving wench, and described as pretty and buxom, has also been reported on more than one occasion.

Dudley

Built on a huge limestone hill, Dudley Castle sits proudly overlooking the ancient town and is one of the highest points in the Black Country. Badly knocked about in the English Civil War by Cromwell's troops, this royalist stronghold is home to many spooks, including the Grey Lady, who, some believe, hung herself, her body swinging to and fro for several hours afterwards from one of the battlements. But there are friendly ghosts too. It is unusual for a ghost to communicate with you, but many people have been acknowledged by an elderly couple who walk the grounds of the castle and zoo, not just at night but in the daylight hours too. Their clothing suggests they are from another time, or perhaps they are guides in historical dress. He may lift his hat, she may nod in your direction, but they both

Dudley Castle.

Dudley Zoo; not just home to animals but ghosts a–plenty too.

disappear before your very eyes. The Grey Lady may be a poor soul who committed suicide, but some say in relation to the birth of a baby and some suggest she is actually Dorothy Beaumont. A monk dressed in black, referred to as the Black Monk, is also seen in and around the vicinity. The same vision is seen in the nearby ruins of St James's Priory, close to the priory estate that originally belonged to a Benedictine order linked to Much Wenlock, who did indeed wear jet-black habits. Reports of historical characters are common, yet, interestingly, the ghosts of a gentleman and lady dressed in the style of the early 1930s, appearing in and around the castle grounds and zoo, have also been seen. My friend, one-time director of tourism, Keith Cheetham, organised ghost walks in this area, but a strange occurrence that seemed to happen whenever I took any of my students on this walk was that many of them seemed to see ghosts that were not actually on the itinerary. Readers of this book who attend any of the various psychic events held at the castle, including overnight stays and present ghost walks, may have the same experiences too.

Dudley

A strange atmosphere, unusual mists and dark figures have all been witnessed by people on the Dudley Ghost Walk whilst in Green Man Alley. Interestingly, the plaque of the Green Man (considered by many to be an ancient fertility figure or a nature spirit) can be seen over the entrance to the alley itself.

Green Man Alley, Dudley.

Dudley

More than one person has reported witnessing a road accident outside Burton Road Hospital, which is not always seen by others present at the same time. The road is strewn with broken glass and fragments of damaged vehicles, and two people can be heard shouting at each other, when suddenly the vision disappears.

Dudley

The Jolly Collier, Holly Hall, was a former inn. The family who lived there for over two years reported seeing a young blonde lady, dressed all in white and wearing distinctive bright lipstick. The shade of a man with a bald head has also been seen. Many unusual noises, bangs and footsteps are reported to come from empty parts of the building. The odd thing about this haunting is that the family said it started suddenly and without warning, and then completely stopped, never to occur again. Could it start again some time in the future? Who can say?

Dudley

Steve Welton told me of a strange experience his family had at the house they lived in at Kate's Hill. They lived there for a four-month period before leaving, during which time they heard the sound of crying babies, slamming doors, objects being moved around of their own accord, and, perhaps the strangest experience of all was when his partner tried to open the door to the cellar and clearly felt it being pulled back from the inside. This happened on four occasions. A visiting medium told the family she could see the bodies of First World War people in the cellar. Was this their way of trying to reach out for help on this side? It certainly needed investigating, and we can only hope that the medium involved did so.

Dudley

The Mount Hall of Residence, situated in Dixon's Green Road, is said to be haunted by the ghost of a beautiful young nun who committed suicide there in the distant past, when it was a convent. Little wonder then that there have been reports of a lady of a religious order walking the street, sometimes with rosary beads in her hands, at other times a rope in her hands. Jean, a sensitive of the old town, felt the nun had an association to the name Mary Magdalene, perhaps a name she took in Confirmation, or perhaps it was just the name Mary that the Dudley medium was picking up?

Dudley

The Swan, on its former site in Castle Street, is a very interesting case. The cellar of this public house is said to be haunted by the ghost of an eighteenth-century public executioner. It is little wonder then that reports were made of a gentleman who seemed to have something in his hand, possibly a rope. Various names have been put forward for this character and, although it may seem humorous, Tom, Dick and Harry were regularly given. It was no joke though when barrels were heard rolling about in the cellar when no one was present.

Dudley

Many people claim the Station Hotel to be one of the Black Country's most haunted pubs, and many investigations by paranormal groups have taken place there. It is also where the Dudley Ghost Walk used to start, when led by Keith Cheetham and his team. The cellars are said to be haunted by a buxom serving wench and a gent in a leather apron. One of the rooms

The Station Hotel, Dudley.

is said to be haunted by a lady from the Victorian period, and some people say they have seen a praying monk in and around the vicinity. It is a fascinating place, that's for sure.

Great Barr

There are regular reports of ghostly happenings at the corner of Chapel Lane and Crook Lane, which include the very faint vision of spectral horses and the sound of strange, and at times quite alarming, screeching and sudden loud bangs, startling people who have not been able to tell where they came from or what they were. These are often reported as happening at dusk or dawn.

Normal or Paranormal?

It is possible these are paranormal experiences and the sounds and visions are of events from yesteryear, but it is always worth considering with such stories that sounds can carry, particularly on the wind. As the visions have tended to be very faint, the possibility of light conditions must be considered to be relevant.

Halesowen

Old Bogs Farm has a very interesting background, for it was said to have been cursed by a witch in 1843, and several people have claimed it has been haunted by many, many ghosts ever since, including the vision of two witches, one known as the Old Hag and one known as Marian the Pretty Witch. Strange as it may seem, legend says it is most fortuitous to see the Old Hag and good luck is coming your way, whereas seeing the Pretty Witch is just the opposite, and, whether you are male or female, you may have romantic difficulties in the near future if you see her.

Holbeache House, Kingswinford.

Kingswinford

Holbeache House is today a nursing home, but in 1605 was very much linked to the gunpowder plot. In and around this area a ghost known as Wombourne's Phantom Horseman has been seen, and the shades of cavaliers and Roundheads are also seen and heard calling to one another. Many people have reported hearing the noise of gunshots in the night or, more appropriately, the crack of the old pistols and muskets they would have used at that time. Certainly shot and cannonballs have been discovered in this area, which tend to reinforce these ghostly replays being possible, for battles did take place here and conspirators, Stephen Lyttleton and Robert Winter, although they escaped, were later captured on nearby Pensnett Chase. You can see how their memories would link them back to Holbeache and its surrounding area.

Kinver

There is an area just a little way from the village known as 'The Compa', which is said to be haunted by the ghost of Old Joe, a former land worker. At one time a local couple, Reg and Jean, were so familiar with Old Joe that they actually set a place for him at the dinner table!

Lye

At the end of Hill Road you will see a large car park, which used to be the site of a house where numerous reports have been made of a ghost appearing, headless and armless. Some years ago, a Welshman claimed it was the ghost of a man who had once lived there. One can only presume that such a vision must have been very disconcerting for anyone who saw it. But could this story link to the present, where the car park is said to be haunted by a very unpleasant character; male, dark and very tall, who has been known to bang on the windows of cars as they leave the car park, but, oddly enough, never when they arrive. If this story is in someway linked to the haunted house on Hill Road, which was demolished many years ago, it would tend to prove that some ghosts still remain even when buildings have long since gone. Some residents of Lye call the ghost 'Blood Stock', others 'Arthur'. I am sure you would agree the latter name certainly sounds the more friendly!

The car park at Lye, said to be haunted by a very unpleasant character.

Netherton

A strange windmill stands in this area where someone told me they had seen the vision of a Viking warrior on the Winter Solstice, or the shortest day of the year, although I found no real evidence to support this possibility. However, it is an unusual area where another correspondent, Mr Taylor, experienced seeing what he described as a large bright glowing light, very low in the sky, which suddenly made a popping sound and vanished. Mr Taylor thought it was more likely to be a UFO than a ghost.

Normal or Paranormal?

A good friend of mine, Barrie Roberts, came up with a possible explanation for what this may have been. It is believed that the movement of underground rock formations sometimes create what is known as electro-magnetic blobs that discharge into the atmosphere and rise from the ground. When the right kind of rocks are moving, apparently they glow in the dark and shine in daylight. Having said that, the appearance of a Viking could not possibly fit in with this explanation, and the bright glowing light could have been a UFO.

Old Hill

Haden Hill House is situated between Halesowen Road and Bars Road in Old Hill and is open to the public. It is said to be a very haunted building, and is believed to stand on the site of an even older Tudor hall. Staff and visitors tell of the White Lady, who floats down the stairs, occasionally blocking the passage of others and creating a sort of energy that holds people back for a few seconds. Some sensitives, who claim they have seen her very clearly, suggests she was of Tudor times, others that her apparel is more Victorian. The building also has other White Ladies, nuns, monks and two girls known as the Grey or White Sisters.

Old Hill

The site of the former Cherry Orchard, close today to Waterfall Lane, is the alleged scene of the ghost of a Scotsman, some name as Andrew, others Old Jock, who was reputedly killed for his gold. He walks the area dressed in seventeenth-century clothing, with a pouch holding his gold attached to his wrist. This has been a well-reported occurrence over the years and the sort of situation, if he was killed there, that causes a replay in the ether than can be seen over and over again by those sensitive to such things.

Portobello, nr Willenhall

The bridge at Neachells Lane has always been described as an unusual place, with spectres that flicker in and out of view and sometimes the sound of an old bus, coach or taxi, which rattles by and stops on the bridge. This has been described as more of an audio experience than a visual one, and some people have found it quite emotional as they have walked down the lane and over the bridge.

Rowley Regis

Tom Johns had a very strange experience one morning while walking on the Rowley Hills. From nowhere he saw falling from the sky what he described as a collection of frogs, some 30yds in front of him. Running to the scene, many of them seemed to have vanished, but a few could still be seen clearly alive, before jumping away and being lost from sight. Tom claims it was not his imagination as he had his Jack Russell terrier with him and she had chased them around. He asks, 'Where did they come from and where did they all vanish to?' Tom came to the conclusion that they were either ghostly in context or he had witnessed some other kind of paranormal event.

Normal or Paranormal?

Mr Johns certainly had a very unusual experience and there is always the possibility that it could have been paranormal. But similar examples of what he experienced have happened before to other people as far back as Biblical times, when whole towns were showered with living creatures such as fish and, indeed, frogs. Some scientists might suggest this was a meteorological phenomenon, possibly caused by the creatures being gathered up or lifted by strong winds passing over water from other nearby land, other parts of the country or even other parts of the world, then, as the wind stilled or dropped, they would be deposited in that exact place.

Rowley Regis

The site of Hales Abbey is haunted by the ghost of a priest who is said to have broken his holy vows by falling in love with a local woman and has been seen walking and praying. A woman is also said to appear wringing her hands and crying.

Sandwell

Medical staff have told me of their scary experiences at Sandwell General Hospital, including doors that are shut fast or feel as though they are being held from the other side, and objects that would move of their own accord. Some nurses also told of leaving the hospital late at night and hearing a strange buzzing sound. One said it sounded like bees swarming, which followed her for a short distance and then seemed to just go back the way it came.

Sedgley

Harry, a retired mechanic and engineer, told me of a rather unnerving experience he used to have in his garage, which he had always believed to be haunted. The building was just an old brick workshop that he had converted to put his car in, but whenever he went

Sandwell Hospital.

to do jobs there, tools seemed to vanish and other objects move. His daughter invited some of her ghost-hunting friends to investigate and film the interior with their video recorder. The group informed Harry that his garage was haunted by an old farmer who had once lived on land there, and who was only trying to help him with his jobs. They also showed him a video and photographs they had taken in the garage, which seemed to show hundreds of orbs and other floating objects.

Normal or Paranormal?

It is an interesting story and it may well be that Harry's garage is haunted by the old farmer. But it is also a fact that 99 per cent of orbs taken with digital cameras prove to be no more than light reflection from various sources. Another point is that if you get a brush and brush it against a wall and then film it with a video camera, you get almost all the unusual floating objects and other things some so-called investigators claim on film. I am not suggesting for one minute that the group who investigated this site did this, but it is a fact that the general public should be aware of. But who moved the tools and other objects? That remains a mystery!

Shelfield, Walsall

Some residents tell of seeing an old-fashioned steam train that runs on railway tracks that are no longer present, with the sound and smell of those old engines permeating the air. This is probably what you would describe as an imprint-type situation that replays in the ether over and over again to those who are sensitive to such things.

Shelfield steam train.

Short Heath, nr Willenhall

Rough Wood Nature Reserve has had many reports of paranormal goings-on, which include the vision of a woman dressed in white and covered with vegetation from the murky waters of the lake, where legend has it she met her end. Some research suggests the lady may have been named Paula or Polly, and that she could be a person who disappeared from the region in the mid-1880s with her young daughter, Evelyn. There could be some truth in this, for in Halesowen for many years there was a tradition at Halloween of dressing up, the ladies at least, in white dresses with pieces of grass, reeds, etc hanging from them. There is also a rhyme that has passed down within the community which goes: 'White Lady, White Lady, come get your babby'. Research does suggest that a Pauline Kelly existed, and also the story of a child being abducted or lost shortly after Pauline's demise. Perhaps this is what keeps her linked to this world long after what appears to have been an awful double tragedy.

Stourbridge

The Oldswinford pub has a ghostly visitor known simply as the Gentleman Ghost. The grey-haired man, dressed in a black suit and top hat, seems to be a regular visitor to the 300-year-old building. Some locals think the vision is rather like the doctor who was in charge of the building before it was converted into a pub in 1970. Many people who drink at this popular hostelry have stories to tell, such as the sounds of shouting voices, buxom wenches, and a short man who carries a black bag. Ann-Marie, the latest of a long line of managers, has experienced unearthly happenings whilst pulling pints for the customers, and locals and staff alike claim that other presences also preside over this Black Country public house, including the ghostly figure of a man.

Smethwick

Black Patch Park is situated in Foundation Lane and has long had the story of an old woman that haunts the area close to the nearby Birmingham Canal. Other stories tell of the spectre of a woman pushing a pram very quickly, so much so that she may overtake you on a quiet stroll and just as quickly dissolve away into nothing. One young man who saw this vision described her as a very pretty lady with long dark hair, not at all scary, and with a wonderful friendly smile. One wonders if this may be the shade of the former queen of the gypsies, Henty, who carried such a description down through her Romany ancestors. Legend also has it that the Romany encampment that was in this park during the time of Henty, loved it very much but may also have cursed it when they were forced to leave the land they considered belonging to them.

Tettenhall, nr Wolverhampton

In Wrottesley Road stands a very large house, which, according to Steve, who worked there at one time, was haunted by the head and shoulders of a lady surrounded by a white mist. Steve said that when you were in the grounds or outside, from one particular part of the house, the lady would peer out from one of the windows above. A little research suggests this may have been an employee who worked at the big house, and for some reason best known to her or the realms of the other world, always seemed to be around to put in a ghostly appearance in the month of July. Some people think this is more common than you would expect, ghosts that appear annually at a certain time, and has something to do with what happened at a particular time that causes it to replay, just as it would have taken place when they were alive.

Tipton

People from all over the country flock to the Black Country Museum to see how people lived in years gone by, but it also has more than its share of ghosts. The Bottle & Glass pub is particularly renowned for its ales, but also has spirits of another kind that put in an appearance on occasions, sometimes behind the bar, other times a gentleman that sits at the piano and tinkles the ivories for those that are not sensitive enough to see him but who can hear the old Joanna as it plays on its own. The bus terminus is also said to have a gentleman ghost. Perhaps the rebuilt buildings have taken the spirits with them from their old homes and sites. It was also at the museum that I was told of the story of William Bury one Halloween, who, according to some Black Country folk, was the real Jack the Ripper. (*See page 17*)

Upper Gornal

Mary Newell of Wolverhampton told me a very interesting story that happened to her in the Coseley and Upper Gornal area. Mary and her friend had been to a public house in Bilston that often sold lots of general items. Whilst there, they noticed two pictures that looked like the Blue Boy and the Gainsborough Lady, which they bought. Mary's friend didn't like the picture of the lady and asked her if she would like to have it, which she did. Taking it home, Mary hung on one of the walls. One day she had to go shopping in Bilston and left her twelve-year-old-son, Jez, painting with his friend Midge, in the

The Bottle & Glass public house, Tipton.

The Black Country
Museum, Tipton.

room in which the painting hung. Returning home, Mary was extremely cross when she noticed that the white dress the lady in her picture was wearing, now had a large red mark down it. Challenging the two boys, Jez pointed out that he would not have been able to do this as he was in a wheelchair and could not reach it, and Midge reassured Mrs M, as he always called her, that he would not do such a thing. Many people who looked at the print saw unusual shapes, faces and people in it. Shortly after this, Mary's friend Kath, whose daughter Pat was moving to keep the Mill pub in Upper Gornal, asked if she had any antiques or old-fashioned items that she could donate to set a historical scene in some of the pub's rooms. Mary kindly donated an old Blunderbuss gun and the Gainsborough Lady picture. As soon as it was hung at the pub, people started to say they could see strange visions in it – one of the favourites being a nun – and other faces, ladies in particular. Very quickly queues were forming to view it at the Mill, and one of the local papers carried a story about it. Mary's friend, who had been with her when they first purchased the pictures, admitted she didn't want the Gainsborough Lady because she felt there was a murder linked to the lady, and that the picture itself was strange. This is one of the most fascinating stories I think I have come across in my many years of investigating the paranormal.

Walsall

The site of the old Bentley Hall is where several reports of a haunting by a spectral cavalier have been made, including Janet Day, who saw what she described as rather like the person in the painting of the Laughing Cavalier. There have also been reports of strange noises, ghostly laughter and a riderless black horse seen in the area in the early hours of the morning and at dusk.

Walsall

Martin Jones told me of a very unusual experience he had of a new car he bought. Martin and his wife had collected a used car from a Rowley Regis garage and parked it outside their flat that evening. Hearing a sound outside during the early hours, his wife roused him from his sleep to say, 'There's someone in the car. I think it's being stolen.' Rushing to the window, Martin could see the car was indeed running as it was a cold night and smoke could be seen coming from the exhaust pipe. The young couple rushed downstairs from their second-floor flat to find the car still there, locked and with no one in sight. Remembering the smoke from the exhaust, Martin felt the pipe expecting to be warm at least, but it was freezing cold. In his words, they never liked that car and they seemed to have nothing but bad luck with it, to the extent they had sold it within six months. Had someone who owned it before them, resented losing the vehicle? Or could a ghost have taken a fancy to their car that evening? This is an unusual story that has happened to other people too, especially of having vehicles that they just didn't feel right with. When you consider that cars have killed more people than the two world wars put together, perhaps there is something to following your intuition if something doesn't feel quite right with it.

Walsall

In 1973, a young man travelling home in the early hours of the morning found his car grinding to a halt in Bentley Lane, with something invisible banging on the windscreen. The same thing happened to another young man in 2007.

Walsall

The Green Dragon public house is an unusual building and old too, for it is mentioned in 1627 when Walsall officially became a town. The building has always been owned by Walsall Council, perhaps quite handy for councillors to take lunch or a tipple! But seriously, one wonders if any other council has ever owned a pub in the UK. It stopped operating as a licensed premises in 1910 and became part of the local magistrates court, but it is currently employed as a pub again. Clare, from the local archivists department, related an interesting story about the pub's funny goings-on. It seems that, for no reason at all, temperatures around the building would drop considerably, while local people say a woman dressed in blue stands looking out of a window on the second floor. You wouldn't be able to check that today, as it has been knocked into one long room and not viewable. The lady ghost is thought to be Mary Hemming, the wife of Deacon Hemming, who bought the pub at one time from the council. The couple were not married long and quickly had three little boys who, according to some research, all sadly passed away within six months of each other. One, little George, is also claimed to be heard on occasions, and also the sounds of infant crying.

Walsall

There is an ancient legend in this old leather-making town that suggests St Matthew's Church was moved and then rebuilt on its present site by the little people or fairy folk. The legend may be rooted in the fact that it seems originally The Chuckery had been the area chosen to be its place of building before a decision was later made to build it in its present position. Charles Poole, in his book *Customs, Superstitions and Legends* of Stafford, says the vicinity according to popular belief is peopled by the little folk who still gambol there. The Black Country and Walsall have always had a strong Irish immigrant population and one can only wonder if the story of the Little People may also have origins from these people. My own wife certainly says that her grandmother always claimed she had seen such people and would not be shaken in this belief.

Walsall

The Town Hall has ghosts both past and present, say staff from the curator's office, who have been witness to a ghostly grey form that moves across the stage and middle of the hall and feel it may be the ghost of the wife of a former curator.

Walsall

The White Hart Inn at Caldmore Green is said to be the site of hauntings of several kinds over many years. Unfortunately, it has been badly damaged by a fire, but of course fire cannot hurt ghosts and there are quite a few to consider, such as a female servant and the background to the so-called 'Hand of Glory'. I have visited this place myself several times and can only describe it as having a very strange atmosphere.

Walsall

The Brewery Stores public house in George Street stands on the site of an old coaching inn known as the Castle. In the late 1990s when the building was developed, many building workers found it difficult to complete their tasks. Tools and building materials would disappear or be strewn about rooms, and on one particularly scary occasion, electric cables were cut and members of the staff and the contractors described poltergeist-type activity such as things flying from one side of the room to the other and of seeing the dark figure of a tall person in a hood. Many parts of the rooms also had cold spots where the temperature suddenly dropped. Several paranormal organisations have investigated the property and have alleged it to be genuinely haunted, although a lot of the happenings seemed to quieten down after the development work was completed in 1998.

Town Hall buildings, Walsall.

Walsall

According to one young man who contacted me, there is a house in Kelvin Road that was haunted by the ghost of an old man who has been known to physically place his hands around the necks of those of whom it would seem he does not feel should be there. Apparently he had done this on a few occasions just as the young man woke up from sleep. The story I was told was that at one time the old chap had lived there with his daughter and they had been very close. Perhaps he was jealous of any young man that might come into her life. In latter years, however, it seems that everything has gone very quiet.

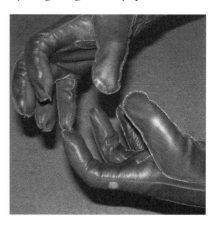

Haunted hands, Kelvin Road, Walsall.

Experts in the field believe that when you first wake up it is difficult to know whether you are still dreaming or whether what you are experiencing is real. This may have been the case for the young man who had this happen to him. Being told the story of the hands could also reinforce the dreaming possibility. There again, many who are knowledgeable in the psychic field, claim that everyone is at their most psychically attuned just as they wake up between the conscious and unconscious state.

Walsall

The Manor Hospital in Moat Street is home to lots of ghosts. Just ask some of the older nurses and they'll tell you stories a-plenty of the grumpy old matron nicknamed The Dragon or perhaps more affectionately referred to as Elizabeth and also of a pretty young nurse. Not so pleasant, is the ward where some nurses experienced a feeling of being pinned down by an unseen force on beds and trolleys. This is a situation that had gone on for some while, but after being asked by staff, with my mediumship we managed to bring this to an end. There are also reports on occasions of a cold wind that zips through the outpatients department and some nurses describe this as being the ghost of Charlie, a former porter who still feels drawn on occasions to help with emergencies. Almost all hospitals have stories of ghosts, and the Manor is no different. A rather nice one that many of the nurses told me, was of patients who spoke of an old-fashioned nurse who visited them in the night and just made them feel so much better and comforted in every way. Other nurses told a similar story of a lady of a religious order they described as a Sister of Mercy or similar who again brought great comfort and never scared the patients. The problem was that the staff knew quite well no visit was ever made by anyone of a living nature. Some more unusual ones include a ghostly ambulance, strange bangs and noises and things being moved without explanation and old-time nurses in period dress putting in what can only be described as unpaid service. Nurses in particular, but other hospital staff as well, are made of pretty stern stuff, but these things naturally scared some of them. I think I helped them all feel a lot better when I explained that as a medium it was all perfectly natural in my view, and even though most of them did reply, 'You've got to be joking, Philip!' I think the reassurance greatly helped.

Walsall

Bith at one time owned a shop in Walsall and had a very unusual experience while driving her car right at the top of Church Hill down towards the town centre. She described what she could only claim was a figure in a sort of transparent or translucent mist rising up and forming into a human-shaped figure in the road ahead of her. Bith felt quite certain that she was witnessing a ghost, but stopped the car and went back to examine the site of where she saw the mist and found that it was in actual fact steam that was rising from a drain in the road. Many other people have had similar visions as this and reported them as being definitely ghostly apparitions. I have included this story because I think it is a good example, if you are brave enough to go and examine a situation as Bith did, you can very often find an answer that has a normal rather than a paranormal explanation to it.

Wednesbury

Wednesbury is an ancient place that was believed to be important to Anglo-Saxon people and also perhaps Vikings. The name Woden clearly has significance in the name of

The author at St Bartholomew's Church, Wednesbury.

Wednesbury. Michael and Jane reported seeing someone similar to a Viking in a helmet, without the horns you would associate with such warriors, near to St Bartholomew's Church on the hill.

Wednesbury

The Anchor Hotel which later became a dance school was reported as being haunted in a interesting story in Carol Arnall's book, *Mysterious Occurrences*, which reads: 'There was a restaurant in Wednesbury called the Anchor. The building is still there but it is something else now. Whether they still have the problems my mother, grandmother and I experienced, I do not know. My mother and another cook were always the first in the building in the mornings and the dumb waiter was always going up and down of its own accord. Although the electricity had been checked regularly, it had not been found to be at fault and it would have needed someone to operate it by pushing the relevant buttons upstairs, but no one was there.' She goes on to say the owner had two large dogs who would not go upstairs. They would also bark and growl at empty spaces and their hackles would go up on end at nothing visible to others, so much so, that they had to be kept in yard and would not even enter the building at all. Doors locked and unlocked themselves or opened of their own accord and Carol reported there was an atmosphere about it that would give you serious goosebumps. I did find this story interesting, and one could only hope it didn't give those learning to do the cha cha cha or the waltz too many problems when it was turned into a dance school.

Wednesbury

There have been numerous reports of a ghostly brown dog that roams the King's Hill area of the town and usually brings a warning of some nature to the people who see it.

Wednesbury

Rebecca told me a very interesting story of a recent Halloween prank that turned scary for the pranksters! She and three friends had heard a legend that if you walked backwards thirteen times around St Bartholomew's Church, the ghost of Freda (or possibly Elthelreda?) would appear to you and grant you a special wish. The girls claim the historical lady did appear to them, but with her head tucked under her arm and that the head spoke the words, 'Go away and let me rest in peace!' Perhaps a little bit of collective hypnosis had taken place here, or maybe someone was dressed in fancy-dress that Halloween evening, a time of trick and treating and the playing of pranks, but one thing Rebecca assured me of, they were more than a little spooked and never tried it again!

Wednesbury

The Black Horse in Old Park Road is a very unusual public house. One time licensee, Sam Lucas, had some very strange experiences there. The very first night of taking it over he stayed there on his own, but was woken up in the middle of the night by his bedroom door loudly slamming shut. Sam was a sensible man and immediately thought there must be some answer to it, but then almost immediately and systematically, every door in the room opened and slammed shut. He had his faithful dog, Brandy, with him but the dog was terrified and would not leave the room under any circumstances. Sam was a brave man and a D-Day veteran and he promised God if he got through that night he would never be afraid of anything else again. Finding courage, he got up and searched the pub from top to bottom. There was no one there at all and more amazingly, each and every door and window was locked tight. A family member said they once saw the ghost of an old-fashioned policeman there and another family member saw what she described as a black moving cloud that formed in a spot just under the hatch to the loft. Investigations made by the family led to them hearing the rumour that an architect had hanged himself in the building at one time. Perhaps that was the reason for all the paranormal goings-on.

Wednesfield

Patricia worked at New Cross Hospital for many years and knew the area well. She told me about some nuns that were regularly seen on various wards and one nun in particular who was seen to walk some of the corridors of the hospital at night. She also told me the story of Old Joe the porter, who would continually move things around and put them in places where you could never find them, then suddenly they would be where you had already looked for them. There is also a story of a young man who is seen saying his prayers, but generally outside the hospital rather than inside the building. Some of the older nurses called him Little John, others Robert, no one really seems to know why he prays or why he would be there at all, but is always considered a pleasant little chap, as are all the ghosts that occasionally join the medical staff and patients at the hospital.

New Cross Hospital, Wednesfield.

Wednesfield

Linda Smith and her friend Carol had a very unusual experience in Wednesfield in the mid-1960s. Both girls were very keen on dancing, particularly pop groups such as the Beatles, Searchers and Billy Fury. Walking close to the New Cross Hospital area at the bottom of the town the girls walked past two young chaps standing by a wall on the bridge, eating chips, on the main road to Wolverhampton. As the girls passed them, the lads wolf-whistled them and called out, 'Hey, would you like some chips?' in an unusual accent that sounded more Liverpudlian than Black Country. Linda admits that both girls thought the lads were very attractive, particularly the tall, blond one who looked a lot like Billy Fury. The other was dark and a resembled a slim Elvis Presley. Carol said to Linda, 'Let's walk back and see if they speak to us again. If they do, let's just say "hello" and see if they chat us up.' Walking back, they could see the two lads clearly, still standing by the wall, but in a playing hard-to-get fashion, the girls crossed the road before reaching them. As they stepped onto the pavement on the opposite side of the road they looked back to let the lads know they might be interested, but they had completely vanished. In Linda's words, there was nowhere they could have gone, the road was clear and there wasn't anywhere for them to be out of view. Thenceforth, the girls believed they'd had an experience of seeing two ghosts. When this story was mentioned by me on a radio programme some years later, a lady telephoned in to say her brother and cousin had been killed in a motorcycle accident in that area and they were what could be described as good-looking Teddy Boy characters and perhaps a bit like Billy Fury and Elvis Presley. The thing that made her

The bridge at Wednesfield.

story particularly interesting though, was when she said her cousin who had been a pillion passenger on her brother's powerful Norton motorcycle came from Liverpool. A strange experience indeed for all concerned.

Wednesfield

Susan had a very unusual experience right in the centre of Wednesfield town. She was driving to work in the late 1970s, when she suddenly realised she had not made sandwiches as she usually did for her husband to take to work with him. He was working shifts in Darlaston, and would have nothing to eat that day if she did not let him know in time, so she parked up and went into a nearby telephone box to call him. Fiddling in her purse for some loose change the telephone suddenly rang three times. She picked up the receiver to answer it. The voice on the other end said, 'I'm sorry, but Susan's not here right now.' You are probably thinking it was just an answerphone machine. It could have been, but they were rare back then and, even stranger, Susan insisted the voice sounded like that of her late grandmother, who had died a few years earlier. She was stunned and dropped the telephone, and, instead of continuing on to work, went straight back home. Pete, her husband, was still fast asleep in bed and rather cross when she woke him up, insisting the telephone never rung. She was puzzled, but got back into her car and drove to work. When she got there though, she couldn't get the experience out of her mind and told her colleagues, who came up with all sorts of answers as to what it could have been. 'I'm going to phone Pete,' she told her friend Jackie, 'and make sure that no one had been in the house

The haunted telephone box, Wednesfield.

or disturbed anything. It wasn't something I thought about when I went back home earlier on.' She wondered if perhaps they had been burgled. After work that night, she decided to pluck up her courage and take another look in the telephone box on the way home. Incredibly, considering the busy position of the telephone box, the receiver still hung from its cord as she had left it. However, as she opened the door the telephone rang three times once more and she could hear the voice from the receiver saying, 'I'm sorry, but Susan's not here right now.' In her words, she slammed the door shut and never used that public telephone box again!

West Bromwich

John South wrote to me about a strange experience that happened to him outside West Bromwich library on a bright, sunny day around midday. He was making his way to the library to change his books when, just as he arrived, an immaculate pink Ford Consul, which he felt would have been from the late 1950s, pulled up. 'That's very nice,' he thought, admiring the model from his earlier years, but then right behind it pulled up what John described as a black Vauxhall Velox or Cresta, with really strange orange headlights and white-walled tyres. 'I forgot the library for a minute,' he said, 'and stood admiring them. They were crystal clear and solid in front of me and I started to make my way towards them to ask the owners if I could have a better look, but before I could even blink they just vanished in front of me.' He said it was not his imagination, he had not been drinking and he had not even been thinking about such vehicles. It is an unusual experience that

A Vauxhall Velox.

John had and one can only wonder why two cars of that era arrived at that spot at that moment. I wondered if they belonged to people that at some time had connections to the library, but no one seems to have any idea about them whatsoever. As for John, he said his experience didn't scare him at all and in fact he sort of enjoyed it.

West Bromwich

The Manor House has long had a history of being haunted, right back to the days when it was simply known as the old hall. Regular reports of a most unusual couple, a gentleman with a dark beard and a white-haired lady, seem to appear on a fairly regular basis. Unusual

The Manor House, West Bromwich.

footsteps and the sound of horses outside have been heard, as have cries and screams from an unknown source. Some research suggests the white-haired lady may be the ghost of a woman who burned to death, either at or near the manor house itself. The restaurant staff in particular seem to have had their fair share of unusual happenings over the years in that part of the building.

West Bromwich

This is another story I was told about telephone boxes. Very close to the library there are two telephone boxes that, a couple of years ago, kept ringing each other alternately. The engineers who worked on them couldn't find any reason or fault to cause it. But perhaps an even stranger experience was when one of my correspondents, Geraldine, stopped to make a call one day. As she entered the box the telephone immediately started ringing. Not quite sure what to do, she left it for a moment before picking up the receiver and saying, 'Hello?' Someone on the other end said, 'Good afternoon, is Geraldine there please?'

'I'm Geraldine,' she replied, 'who are you?' To which the voice again asked, 'Is Geraldine there please?' Quite alarmed, she put the receiver down and left the box, but, looking across to the other telephone box, which was opposite, she could hear that it was ringing. She didn't use the box and didn't answer the call either, and who could blame her? Among the telecom staff the story somehow got round that the telephone boxes were haunted. Who can say for sure that they are not?

The telephone boxes that rang each other in West Bromwich.

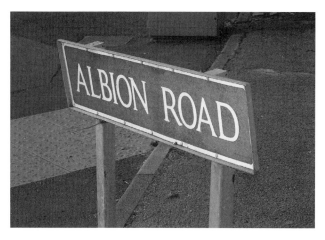

Albion Road, Willenhall.

Willenhall

There is a house situated in Albion Road that made national news a few years ago when the people living there reported themselves as being the victims of poltergeist activity. Sometimes a home is just not right for some people, and yet for others it is just fine. This seems to be the case with this particular property and is the reason it is included as an example of such a case. The people who suffered the haunting at this property are people I know to be quite honest and genuine, and didn't enjoy their stay there one little bit. Who would? However, apparently there are no such difficulties with the present residents at the property.

The Locksmith's House, Willenhall.

Willenhall

Scott Edgerton and Gaynor Cook wrote to me after reading my request for stories in the *Express & Star*. Scott and Gaynor had visited the Locksmith's House in Willenhall on 28 April 2007, and had taken part in a séance in one of the rooms. As Scott glanced up and looked through the door into the next room, he saw someone in a long black or grey dress, with lace around her neck and her hair tied up. She seemed to him to have a very straight back and walked with her hands in front of her. Scott felt he was looking at her through a light heat haze, but could still see her in great detail. When he mentioned his experience to the people running the event, he was informed there was no one in the room at that particular time. Later in the evening, when it became dark, he and his girlfriend stood in a different room holding hands during another séance, and Scott got the feeling that someone was standing behind him trying to look into the circle over his shoulder. He says he looked to the medium, who said he had just seen something. A few minutes later his girlfriend saw a figure walking towards her inside the circle, which she described as a dark shape with no features; no eyes, nose or mouth. She closed her eyes, and when she opened them again the figure was gone. Could it be that this lovely little museum has workers still filing levers and manufacturing locks to this day, but relevant to another world, time and place?

Willenhall

The old churchyard in Wood Street can be a spooky place to walk through late at night or in the early hours of the morning. A young boy and his friends had a very frightening experience here when, from behind one of the old gravestones stepped a figure wearing a bear's head. The person who told me this story didn't realise it was wrong to be playing in such a sacred place, but after this vision neither he nor his friends played there again! Was it some individual's way of scaring the boys off?

Above, right: Artist's impression of the man with the bear's head. (Courtesy of Graham Walsh)

The graveyard in Willenhall, where the boys saw a man with a bear's head.

Ye Olde Toll House
Restaurant, Willenhall.

Willenhall

Next door to Ye Olde Toll House Restaurant is a place that seems to have unusual happenings. Harold Jones told me of the unusual experience of seeing bright lights and the smell of fire. A little research suggests this is possibly the shade of an old forge or blacksmith's shop that was in this area and the lights, that looked like welding lights, may have been sparks from molten metal being hammered into shape, although Janice who lived close by, also told me of seeing gold and silver balls in and around this area one night around dusk as she was making her way round the corner to cut up into nearby Gipsy Lane.

Willenhall

Right at the bottom of the town stands Dr Tonks' Clock, where more than one person has seen people standing in clothes of yesteryear with books in their hands, happily singing Christmas carols around Christmas-time. Others have seen a man with horses and a small boy. An unusual haunting this one, which only seems to be seen by people with great sensitivity or mediumistic ability.

Willenhall

At the top of the town stands the old Central Boys School. One of the caretakers that worked there many years ago told me the story of a young boy who was regularly seen by the staff, dressed in the uniform of the school and there is a story that he may have been killed in an accident with a tram or trolley bus. School was very hard and strict in those days, but if this is the case then this is one little boy who must have actually liked school! Another story tells of a shade of yesteryear dressed in traditional schoolmaster's robes and with a very posh voice that quietly speaks words that you can never quite hear, a bit like the old radios when they weren't properly tuned into the station.

Willenhall

The Dale House Restaurant is situated in an old eighteenth-century townhouse in the heart of Willenhall. The building dates back to 1750 and still has all the original doors and

Dr Tonks' Clock, Willenhall.

famous locks manufactured in this famous town of Willenhall and adjoins the building that was at one time was the town's newest cinema after the old picture house was knocked down. The house was in the ownership of the Hincks family, wealthy local farmers who developed a business in malting. The building eventually became a cinema known as The Dale which had its own story of a teenage girl whose ghost often ran from the building and up into the town and also of a tall figure of a man who was seen to sit in one of the cinema seats, but later was nowhere to be seen. It later became a bingo hall but the hauntings still continued. Tales of the spectre of a Teddy Boy and a black cat that came from nowhere and just as quickly vanished, have long been associated with the building. When Mike was there, as a restaurant it always had a friendly atmosphere but also had its own ghost which favoured the upstairs regions, and, in the words of the staff, liked to 'shimmy across the landing'. Do the ghosts still enjoy the site today, in the restaurant perhaps, with or without a spoon? That is the question.

Willenhall

Behind Temple Road is an area of rough land the locals call The Summers. It was here that Steve Cashwell saw strange glowing lights, which may have been gases rising up from the ground. However, other people have also seen unusual collections of glowing lights, and what have been described as gold or silver balls that hovered in the air. Reg, a local man, informed me he had been told when he was a little boy that ghosts are said to walk where The Summers is, and this may be relevant to the story that there were so many victims of the cholera epidemic that had once blighted Willenhall it had caused the traditional burial grounds to be full to overflowing and meant that many poor people had been buried on land where the Summers are today. Having researched this possibility, I don't seem to be able to find any evidence to suggest this is correct, but Reg was adamant the information about this given to his forefathers was true and that burials did take place there. Some Spiritualists and sensitives believe that collections of globes or lights bunched together can be of spirits or perhaps ghosts and I suppose if they were not properly put to rest, this could be the cause of such visitations taking place. It is strange that they have never built houses

The Summers, Willenhall.

on this piece of land, which one would have thought would have been ideal for such a development. There again, perhaps people wouldn't want to live on such a site.

Willenhall

Ken told me a very interesting story of spooky goings-on in Gipsy Lane, where the old BRS haulage company had stood. Apparently it was quite common for the men who worked there at night to report the sounds of rock'n'roll music ringing out in the air. Some of the workers say that they even saw teenagers dressed in rock'n'roll-style clothing, the sounds of loud motorcycles revving up, and sometimes the sounds of lads fighting and being egged-on by others. One of the drivers, making his way to the BRS late one night, saw two Teddy Boys dressed in brightly-coloured drape jackets walking up Gipsy Lane near to the BRS. As he had heard about the strange things that happened in the area, he stopped his lorry, but nothing was to be heard or seen – the street was empty! I was very interested in this story because, in the late 1950s, my father used to organise record hops at a place called the Toc H Club in Gipsy Lane, and just the sort of teenagers that were described used to come to his rock'n'roll dances. Many had motorcycles and dressed in the way the BRS people described, and, on occasions, Teddy Boys would be involved in fights. Do some of the old memories still come through occasionally, allowing these people to 'rock on'?

Willenhall

A local writer who lived near to Willenhall Park in 1990 told me a very interesting experience he had while writing his latest book. Having difficulties with his hands, this author often favoured the use of a dictation machine. One evening, while working on his latest effort, he left his machine on. The next day, after playing the tape back, everything was blank except for one part, where a voice with a strong cockney accent exclaimed, 'Oh my Gawd!' At a later date, while discussing the recording, one of his neighbours said, 'That's really strange, the man who used to live in your house had a very strong Cockney accent, and although it was probably thirty years before when he lived there, he would answer almost everything with, "Oh my Gawd!"' Whether this ghost was impressed with the content of the author's work no one can say, but I don't think the writer ever left his machine running again!

Willenhall

There is a house in Gipsy Lane that is said to be haunted by the ghost of a miner and many other friendly ghosts. Strangely enough, there is a long-standing rumour that anyone who lives in this house will later go on to have great success in their life, one way or another. When this story was first told in another book, Jill got in touch to say that there was a story that a kindness had been shown to gypsies from the residents of this house, and that was relevant to the good luck story. Residents on both sides of the lane also speak of a ghost train, where the sound of a heavy steam train of yesteryear, together with the smell of such an engine, rock the houses for a few moments as it passes by.

Willenhall

I was personally called in to investigate the Alcatraz nightclub after numerous male and female ghosts were reported being seen. Unusual lights were reported to flash across the floor and some ladies sensed a male presence in the women's toilets. Most disconcerting one would imagine. In the past the upstairs building had been St Mary's Catholic Social Club, and had long had a history of the 'dark man' who would be seen in quieter times.

Alcatraz Rock Club, Willenhall.

Willenhall

Some years ago, two young lads, Tom and Patrick, attended the old St Thomas More Catholic School in Bilston Lane, Willenhall. During a break in lessons they had gone to an area of the school which they really shouldn't have been in at that time, the school chapel. Sitting outside the chapel, all was well to start with, when suddenly the area in front of the boys seemed to be on fire, the ground iridescent with the ever-changing colours of recently extinguished embers. Needless to say, the pair were very alarmed by this experience, but could it have been a time slip? Did they see the remains of a fire that had happened in the past in that particular area? The school has now moved to another location and private houses have been built on the site where the two lads had their experience. One can only wonder if at some time other people have had this same experience, or perhaps will do so in the future. I believe both young men are sensible and genuine in their report of what happened during their days as pupils at the school.

Wollescote

On Oldnall Road, between Wollescote and Cradley, the ghost of a girl is said to appear that may be the cause of accidents and crashes. Some reports suggest she is a little girl, aged about four, and dressed in Victorian attire. Several people have reported literally having to stand on their brakes to emergency stop, or swerve their vehicles around the little girl who suddenly appears in front of them from nowhere. On one occasion a couple saw such a child dressed in dark Victorian clothes, but say she was also with a boy of about eight years of age. A strange experience to say the least.

Wolverhampton

BBC Midlands Today ran a very interesting news feature in 2002, which they called 'The House That Cries'. Graisley Old Hall is one of Wolverhampton's oldest buildings, believed to have been erected in 1485, although some historians suggests the present building may have remnants dating back to 1377. The first residents of Graisley Old Hall were the Rydleys, a family of rich merchants. Ownership later moved to the Rotton family, and later to the Normansells, until it was purchased by the Royal Wolverhampton School for outbuilding use. It was made a listed building in 1957, much through the prompting of famous MP, Enoch Powell. In the past unexplainable pools of water have been reported to appear from nowhere on the floor of the main hall, and visitors have claimed to hear the sounds of dripping or splashing water when nothing visual of such a nature was to be seen. Interestingly, a few years ago a couple told me of a strange grey mist that swirled in front of them within the vicinity of the house, and seemed to have the vision of a young boy within it playing with a spinning top and stick. The water experiences – which only happened four or five times – may well have been due to the type of damp that tends to build up in such houses. Nevertheless, I am sure you can understand why the media became interested in this unusual story.

Wolverhampton

The magnificent Grand Theatre is where the ghost of Mr Purdey, a friendly former manager, is very often seen, along with the sweet perfume of a lady in grey. One member of staff also told me that in the bar area glasses get moved, people get tapped on the shoulder, and the old-fashioned fragrance of lavender has been known to waft in and around the area. Numerous artists who have known nothing of these ghosts have described exactly what I have outlined for you.

The Grand Theatre, Wolverhampton, *c.* 1990.

The Grand Theatre today.

Wolverhampton

Beacon Radio, or WABC as it was known, in Tettenhall Road, has long been known as a strange place to those who have spent time working there. One of the presenters claimed the building was incredibly haunted and that the voices of children were often heard. It is hardly surprising, as at one time historians believe it was an orphanage, and before that an old chapel. Some of the staff have also seen a pretty little girl who sits by the fireside, or in a chair, and those who have broadcasted late into the evening claim to have seen an elderly woman walking up the stairs carrying a tray. Another presenter saw an old lady standing in front of the photocopier. One can only wonder why she would be drawn to that type of equipment. Perhaps she was wondering what in the world it could be!

Wolverhampton

The Central Library is said to have more than its fair share of ghosts; unseen helpers who alter or change things round to suit themselves and regularly put books back where they used to be rather than where they should go now. Some members of staff do not like being in the building on their own, when unexplainable things happen such as books falling from shelves, floors creaking and a spooky feeling of someone standing behind them. One of the girls who worked there some years ago, said she often heard the voice of an older sounding gentleman, who would quietly utter, 'Tut, tut, tut,' behind her.

Wolverhampton

The Civic Hall is probably one of the city's most haunted venues and has a long history of unusual goings-on, as does the adjoining Wulfruna Hall's Green Room. Historians and archivists have found research that suggests the building was built on the original site of the town morgue, and both buildings have had reports of unusual figures seen by staff

Wolverhampton Central Library.

The Civic Hall, Wolverhampton.

and visitors, together with unexplainable sudden bangs or voices from unseen sources. One of the strangest occurrences happened a few years ago, when the rock band Gun were booked in to do a show at the Civic Hall. Before the show started, one of the lighting operators, who was alone in the gallery setting up equipment, repeatedly felt someone or something tapping him on the shoulder. This happened again during the concert, and the lighting operator left the building and the concert, telling the Civic Hall's manager, Mark Blackstock, 'I'm not going back up there again!' And he didn't! Other people have shared the experience of being tapped on the shoulder, and shadows are seen to come from a particular cupboard, together with various perfumes and odours. The cleaners in particular do not like to go near that cupboard if at all possible. There have also been reports from pop bands who have played at the venue, sensing people on stage that were nothing to do with them and were, it would seem, not of this world.

Wolverhampton

Several people have reported seeing the spectre of a large speeding lorry that hurtles down Castlecroft Lane, close to the Staffordshire and Worcester Canal. Several drivers have reported having to pull into the side of the road to avoid a head-on collision, turning to look as the lorry passes by, which then simply dissolves into thin air.

Wolverhampton

The Best Western Connaught Hotel on the Tettenhall Road has always been one of the city's best-loved hotels, not only has it been the temporary accommodation for some incredibly famous people over the years, it is noted for its entertainment events, discos and welcoming atmosphere. The Connaught, as it known, is said to be haunted by several ghosts. Staff have reported seeing strange mists and hearing unusual noises, while objects move around of their own accord and glasses rattle at the bar when no one is near them. According to the present management, one particular ghost to put in an appearance is the hotel's former owner and baron, Sir Harmer-Nicholls, who is always considered friendly and pleasant, not scary in any way. The son of a Walsall miner, he also served in Burma, and later as a councillor and Chairman of Darlaston Council. He was much admired in Wolverhampton, and is said to have held the Connaught in great affection. His daughter is, of course, the actress Sue Nicholls, who has starred in several soap operas, but is best known for her role as Audrey Roberts in ITV's *Coronation Street*. Ironically, she also appeared in *Rent a Ghost*.

Wolverhampton

Several disused railway lines in the town are home to the ghost of a huge brown-coloured cat – described by some as being rather like a Scottish wildcat – which appears from nowhere, spits and hisses at humans, and even attacks dogs. It is unusual for a cat to go on the attack without provocation, but even more unusual is the fact that this one appears from nowhere and just as quickly vanishes into thin air.

A photograph of a Scottish wild cat similar perhaps to the one seen on the disused railway station in Walverhampton.

Wolverhampton

In the late 1860s the town suffered from an unusual manifestation of pebbles falling from the sky in such a large quantity that workmen were required to collect and remove them in some places of the town. This alone is unusual, but there are also reports that in the 1960s some residents of Tettenhall had a similar experience. It's bad enough being stoned in the first place, but from where or what did these objects originate?

Wolverhampton

St John's Vaults public house was alleged to have a ghost known as the Blue Woman. Some say this poor woman leapt to her death from the roof or upper area of the building, and her shade, still wearing the pale blue dress she died in, can be seen around the property at certain times of the year, usually when it is either very cold or very warm. Some people also claimed to have heard spooky footsteps that sound rather light of foot; the way a lady would sound if she were walking barefoot. Could this also be the Blue Woman?

Wolverhampton

In 1972, the Stag's Head public house experienced a number of spooky occurrences. Spectres were seen walking around the cellars on a fairly regular basis, and the beer taps turned themselves on or off without explanation. At one time this happened in excess of twenty times in the same month. Research suggests that changes made to the building may have helped to move the entities on, for the current owners do not seem to have faced the same haunting in recent years.

Wolverhampton

After his defeat at the Battle of Worcester in 1651, the then future king, Charles II, had to flee the area. Many know of the story of the evening spent in the oak tree at Boscobel House, a site that is said to have energies that unnerve or make sad the sensitives among us. It is also claimed the future king was hidden under the floor of Moseley Old Hall, terrified as Cromwell's men marched around above searching for him. The attic at the Old Hall was originally a little chapel. Many today claim it is a foreboding place that puts some visitors on edge. Ghostly cats and a spaniel have also been sighted in and around the rooms. Things go missing then turn up again, and ladies and gentlemen a-plenty, shades from another time, have been reported over the years. One would like to think that one of them could be King Charles, or Black Country heroine Lady Jane Grey of Bentley, Walsall, who helped lead him away from those searching for him in the area to what proved to be the 'safe houses' at Boscobel and Moseley Old Hall.

Wolverhampton

It is a fact that many people of Irish stock made their home in the Black Country and nearby Birmingham too. The twins who told me of this story are as Irish as you could possibly imagine; fair of skin with bright red hair. Bridie and Jenny had both been taught of the legend of the banshee by their parents. They explained to me that they once heard the howling of the banshee and seen a swirling mist outside their house, and instantly felt that someone was very ill or about to pass. The next day the girls' grandmother, Kitty, had indeed left this world. The girls explained to me that in Celtic origin, the banshee is also the Bean Si, the woman of the other world, and the woman of the hills, a Gaelic legend that tells of the forecoming death of someone that has the Isle of Erin within their bloodline.

Wolverhampton

There have been reports of horses that inexplicably appear galloping down Steelhouse Lane, before suddenly disappearing into thin air. Malcolm, a local resident, told me his father used to call it Mighty Mick's Ponies, and that they were relevant to a character who at one time in that area was something of a horse dealer, or perhaps stealer, according to his dad.

Wolverhampton

The Old Molineux Alley (now demolished) was where several people reported seeing a young boy dressed in clothes of the early 1950s, wearing a Wolves scarf and carrying one of the rattles popular at the time, always appearing in a slight mist. Nothing was heard of this lad until 2008, when Rick told me he had been alarmed when walking past the new Molineux to see a very similar vision, although not by his girlfriend who was with him. One wonders if the great days are returning for the Molineux Giants and the lad has decided to return too, in spirit at least. Following the publication of other books, correspondents have suggested to me that the ghost was well known years ago and nicknamed Little Johnny.

Wolverhampton

A lot of the older churches in the Black Country feature stone figures known as gargoyles. These must surely be the answer on occasions to what some people, when they have looked up and caught a glimpse of them in the dusk, have described as scary figures. Take a look at this picture and I think you will see what I mean!

Gargoyles in the Black Country.

Wombourne

A very interesting photograph came into my possession from a lady's wedding day. On one of the graves at the side of the bride is a face that can clearly be seen smiling. Perhaps even more pleasing is that the bride's family are quite sure it is the vision of her elder sister. Had the photographer inadvertently produced a spirit or ghost on film? I actually have this picture in my private collection and it is very interesting indeed. A little more research may perhaps reveal that other images have been seen on gravestones at this Wombourne churchyard. There may be a scientific answer to this image, something to do with light perhaps? Then again, it could be that those who have passed on do visit their final resting places or attend such ceremonies as weddings and baptisms. As a medium, I believe that they do.

Wordsley

Kath told me of her experience working as a nurse at Wordsley Hospital after the Second World War. Working in an area known as H Block, which had three levels, she once had a most incredible paranormal experience. One evening on the second level, while sitting with friends having a break from the strenuous twelve-hour shifts the nurses worked in those days, she suddenly saw for a second the figure of a man beside her, which the girl sitting next to her also clearly saw, but what particularly shocked Kath was that she immediately recognised the person as someone she had nursed in the past and who wasn't living now. She knew it was the former postmaster at Eve Hill post office in Sedgley. She even recognised his very distinctive curly grey hair. He was gone in an instant, but she had no doubt that she saw him. The top floor also had unusual occurrences. This was a place where the nurses would be allowed to take a break and catch a nap on one of the beds. One of Kath's colleagues had the startling experience one night of being turfed out of the bed, and not by hands of this world! It would appear that Wordsley Hospital has many a spooky tale to tell, and these are just two fascinating stories that are part of its ghostly history.

THE END . . . OR IS IT?

The author on the hunt for ghosts.

BIBLIOGRAPHY & REFERENCES

BOOKS

Bradford, Anne, *The Haunted Midlands*, Brewin Books Ltd, 2006
Bradford, Anne and Roberts, Barrie, *Midland Ghosts and Hauntings*, Quercus Books, 1994
Perrins, Andrew B., *Ghosts and Folklore around Barr Beacon*, A.B. Perrins, 2001
Tump, Aristotle, *Black Country Ghosts and Mysteries*, A Bugle Publication, 1987
Smith, Arthur and Bannister, Rachel, *Haunted Birmingham*, Tempus Publishing Ltd, 2006

WEBSITES

www.paranormaldatabase.com
www.bbc.co.uk/blackcountry/stories
http://en.wikipedia.org/wiki/Black_Country#History

OTHER

Mary Bodfish, *Strange Tales from Smethwick*
Carol Arnall, *Mysterious Occurrences*, Lulu.com

Other titles published by The History Press

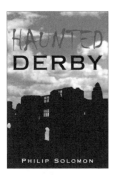

Haunted Derby
PHILIP SOLOMON

This creepy collection of true-life tales takes the reader on a tour through the streets, cemeteries, alehouses and attics of Derby city. Drawing on historical and contemporary sources and containing many tales which have never before been published, it unearths a chilling range of supernatural phenomena from poltergeists to Victorian spirits.

978 0 7524 4484 0

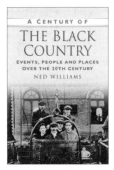

A Century of the Black Country
NED WILLIAMS

This fascinating selection of photographs offers an insight into the daily lives and living conditions of local people and gives the reader glimpses and details of familiar places during this century of unprecedented change. Many aspects of the Black Country's recent history are covered, famous occasions and individuals are remembered, and the impact of national and international events is witnessed.

978 0 7509 4943 9

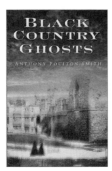

Black Country Ghosts
ANTHONY POULTON-SMITH

Contained within the pages of this book are strange tales of spectral sightings, active poltergeists and restless spirits appearing in streets, inns, churches, estates, public buildings and private homes across the Black Country. They include the ghost of a murdered woman in Dudley's Station Hotel cellar, the tragic lovers of Cradley Heath's Haden Estate, Walsall's notorious 'Hand of Glory' and Coseley's enormous black dog forecasting death.

978 0 7509 5044 2

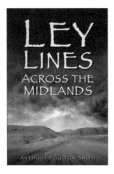

Ley Lines Across the Midlands
ANTHONY POULTON-SMITH

Some maintain that ley lines are the result of some 'earth force', others that they are the earliest routes marked out across the land. In his new book Anthony Poulton-Smith examines the origins and meanings of these ancient trackways, tracing them on foot and taking in markers that have been in existence for millennia to travel in a straight line from Shropshire and Gloucestershire in the west to Cambridgeshire and Lincolnshire in the east.

978 0 7509 5051 0

Visit our website and discover thousands of other History Press books.www.thehistorypress.co.uk